"Heroes and Villains of Finance *provides a fascinating*
personalities and developments that have transformed
so. Anyone trying to understand where finance is now,
it might go should read this book."

Dr Ste

"An ex   ies
that h

Sam F

"This   tly
celebr   he
poten   we
are in

Profe   rial
Colle   nic
entre

HEROES & VILLAINS OF FINANCE: THE 50 MOST COLOURFUL CHARACTERS IN THE HISTORY OF FINANCE

A BALDWIN

WILEY

This edition first published 2015
© 2015 A Baldwin

Registered office
John Wiley & Sons Ltd, The Atrium, Southern Gate, Chichester, West Sussex, PO19 8SQ,
United Kingdom

For details of our global editorial offices, for customer services and for information about
how to apply for permission to reuse the copyright material in this book please see our
website at www.wiley.com.

Wiley publishes in a variety of print and electronic formats and by print-on-demand. Some
material included with standard print versions of this book may not be included in e-books
or in print-on-demand. If this book refers to media such as a CD or DVD that is not included
in the version you purchased, you may download this material at http://booksupport.wiley
.com. For more information about Wiley products, visit www.wiley.com.

Library of Congress Cataloging-in-Publication Data
Baldwin, A.,
    Heroes and villains of finance : the 50 most colourful characters in the history of
finance/A. Baldwin.
       pages cm
    Includes bibliographical references.
    ISBN 978-1-119-03899-3 (paperback)
    1. Finance—History. I. Title.
    HG171.B36 2015
    332.092′2—dc23   2015006402

A catalogue record for this book is available from the British Library.

ISBN 978-1-119-03899-3 (paperback)   ISBN 978-1-119-03901-3 (ebk)
ISBN 978-1-119-03900-6 (ebk)   ISBN 978-1-119-03902-0 (obk)

Cover design: Wiley
Cover image: © Ollyy/Shutterstock

Set in 11/14pt Myriad Pro-Regular by Aptara, New Delhi, India
Printed in Great Britain by TJ International Ltd, Padstow, Cornwall, UK

CONTENTS

"I AM WORRIED ABOUT OUR TENDENCY TO OVER INVEST IN THINGS AND UNDER INVEST IN PEOPLE."

ECONOMIST JOHN KENNETH GALBRAITH, 1908–2006

01 THALES OF MILETUS

C.624–546 BC

Bertrand Russell once famously said that "Western philosophy begins with Thales". Does Western finance also? Although more renowned for his philosophy and mathematics, the pre-Socratic Greek philosopher Thales was an active figure in business in his town of Miletus. Known as one of the seven sages of Greece Thales of Miletus provides us with the earliest known example of what we now know as options trading…

…One autumn, Thales predicted that favourable weather the following year would result in an above average harvest and so during the winter he negotiated with local olive press owners for the option to exercise the right to use a number of olive presses in Miletus the following year. When spring arrived, his weather forecast proved correct, upon which he exercised his 'options' before proceeding to rent out the olive presses at a much higher price than what he paid.

With this, the 'option' was born.

Whilst today, the 'option' industry has developed into a vast, complex market, its underlying reasoning remains the same as it was when Thales conceived it: an instrument that grants the holder the right (but not the obligation) to engage in a specific transaction, at a specific time, for a specific price.

"...FOR THEY SAY THAT HE [THALES], PERCEIVING BY HIS SKILL IN ASTROLOGY THAT THERE WOULD BE GREAT PLENTY OF OLIVES THAT YEAR, WHILE IT WAS YET WINTER, HAVING GOT A LITTLE MONEY, HE GAVE EARNEST FOR ALL THE OIL WORKS THAT WERE IN MILETUS AND CHIOS, WHICH HE HIRED AT A LOW PRICE, THERE BEING NO ONE TO BID AGAINST HIM..."

...BUT WHEN THE SEASON CAME FOR MAKING OIL, MANY PERSONS WANTING THEM, HE ALL AT ONCE LET THEM UPON WHAT TERMS HE PLEASED; AND RAISING A LARGE SUM OF MONEY BY THAT MEANS, CONVINCED THEM THAT IT WAS EASY FOR PHILOSOPHERS TO BE RICH IF THEY CHOSE IT."

ARISTOTLE ON THALES, FROM THE POLITICS OF ARISTOTLE

02 CHANAKYA

C.370–283 BC

As the 'pioneer economist of India', Chanakya was one of the earliest and greatest contributors ever to the development of economics and political science. Living c. 370–283 BC, Chanakya was a professor of political science at the Takshashila University, and was later to become the chief architect of the Mauryan empire.

Often referred to as the 'Indian Machiavelli', Chanakya compiled many of his economic and political ideas into his book *Arthashashtra,* which due to its harsh political pragmatism is widely considered a precursor to Machiavelli's *The Prince.* Standing as arguably the first systematic book on economics, the *Arthashashtra* discusses numerous theories, such as monetary and fiscal policies, welfare and ethics, economic management, international relations and war strategies. Many of the topics that Chanakya introduced in the book are still prevalent in modern economics.

Chanakya believed in the power of an autocracy for effective management of an economy, with a solid legal system needing to be observed in order for an economy to thrive.

Perhaps the first person to visualize the concept of a 'nation', Chanakya's teachings offer a bureaucratic framework for the management of a society. Chanakya taught that *'artha'* (sound economies) has paramount importance for the duties and obligations of a king.

> "HENCE THE KING SHALL BE EVER ACTIVE IN THE MANAGEMENT OF THE ECONOMY. THE ROOT OF WEALTH IS [ECONOMIC] ACTIVITY AND LACK OF IT [BRINGS] MATERIAL DISTRESS. IN THE ABSENCE OF [FRUITFUL ECONOMIC] ACTIVITY, BOTH CURRENT PROSPERITY AND FUTURE GROWTH WILL BE DESTROYED."
>
> *CHANAKYA FROM THE ARTHASHASTRA*

Legend has it that one night whilst working Chanakya was visited by a Chinese traveller. Chanakya immediately extinguished the oil lantern that he was working with and lit another. When the Chinese traveller asked if it was an Indian custom to do so, Chanakya is said to have responded "No my dear friend. There is no such custom. Actually, when you entered, I was working. It was an official work, pertaining to my empire, my nation. The oil filled in that lamp has been bought from the money from the National Treasury. Now, I am talking to you. This is a personal and friendly conversation, not related to my nation; so I cannot use the lamp now, as it will lead to wastage of the money of the National Treasury. Hence, I extinguished that lamp and lit this other lamp, since the oil in this lamp has been bought from my personal money."

"TAXATION SHOULD NOT BE A PAINFUL PROCESS FOR THE PEOPLE. THERE SHOULD BE LENIENCY AND CAUTION WHILE DECIDING THE TAX STRUCTURE. IDEALLY, GOVERNMENTS SHOULD COLLECT TAXES LIKE A HONEYBEE, WHICH SUCKS JUST THE RIGHT AMOUNT OF HONEY FROM THE FLOWER SO THAT BOTH CAN SURVIVE. TAXES SHOULD BE COLLECTED IN SMALL AND NOT IN LARGE PROPORTIONS."

CHANAKYA FROM THE ARTHASHASTRA

03 THE KNIGHTS TEMPLAR
C.1119–1314

The Knights Templar were a medieval Christian military organization, officially endorsed by the Catholic Church to provide a pivotal role in protecting pilgrims on their journey to visit the Holy Lands.

Despite the traditional imagery of the Knights Templar, the military face of the organization was actually relatively small; the vast majority of the organization existed to support the knights and to manage the financial infrastructure of the network.

Whilst the Templars themselves were sworn to poverty, due to their extensive sponsors (comprised of nobility and royalty across Europe), within the organization they controlled vast amounts of money throughout Europe.

However, what most people don't realize, aside from the images of swords, horses and crusades, is that the Knights Templar were actually the pioneers of multinational banking.

Many aristocratic figures wishing to participate in the Crusades would entrust the Templars with their wealth whilst they were away. In return, the Templars would issue a 'letter of credit' for the pilgrims. The vast network of Templars stretching across Europe and to the Holy Lands allowed the system to function efficiently. The pilgrims would deposit their valuables with a local Templar before departure, receiving a document indicating the value of their deposit, which they would then use upon arrival in the Holy Lands to retrieve their funds. In addition, by not carrying their wealth on their person whilst travelling, the Pilgrims were less susceptible to being robbed. Essentially, this was an early form of banking, and was quite possibly the first formal system to support the use of cheques.

As a result, the vast network of Templars was able to acquire large holdings of land across Europe and the Middle East, build churches and castles, and engage in various import and export activities. With up to 20,000 members at its peak, they even had their own fleet of ships. The network they developed, and the way in which they operated, is widely regarded to be the first example of a multinational banking corporation.

AT ONE POINT, THE KNIGHTS TEMPLAR OWNED THE ENTIRE ISLAND OF CYPRUS

LEGEND HAS IT THAT THE KNIGHTS
TEMPLAR WERE THE PROTECTORS
OF THE 'HOLY GRAIL'...

... ALTHOUGH THE IDENTITY OF THE 'HOLY GRAIL'
IS STILL DISPUTED – MANY BELIEVE IT TO BE
THE CHALICE JESUS DRANK FROM AT THE
LAST SUPPER, OTHERS CONSIDER IT TO BE THE
SHIPPING ROUTES TO THE ORIENT, WHILST SOME
SAY IT WAS THEIR ORGANIZATIONAL STRUCTURE
OF THEIR MULTINATIONAL BANK.

04 NICOLE ORESME

C.1320–1382

Undoubtedly one of the greatest economic thinkers of the middle ages, the European roots of the quantity theory of money originate from the workings of Nicole Oresme.

Born in Normandy (France) around 1320, Oresme studied theology, and eventually rose to become Bishop of Lisieux, and chaplain and advisor to King Charles V.

Oresme lived throughout a period of great financial upheaval in France; unlike the contemporary relative stability of many Western currencies, French monarchs freely manipulated their currency for personal gain. For example, between 1295 and 1305 the value of the French currency was reduced by 80%, subsequently to return to its original value in the following decade and then to fall once again the next decade.

Thus, much of Oresme's work deals with his concerns about the persistent, aggressive and arbitrary changes to the value of money resulting from successive devaluations by the French ruling classes for their own personal gain.

As the author of the first independent, comprehensive economic thesis, Oresme represents a key milestone in the development of early economic literature.

His thesis provided the first statement on the quantity theory of money, taking inspiration from the monetary policies of his contemporary French monarchs. Oresme condemned devaluations and instead highlighted the importance of maintaining the perceived value of the national currency in order to provide stability.

ORESME'S LEGACY WAS SEALED WHEN HE OUTLINED THAT THE RULING MONARCH HAD A DUTY TO THEIR NATION TO ACT AS PROTECTOR (AS OPPOSE TO OWNER) OF THEIR NATIONAL CURRENCY

LAYING THE FOUNDATIONS FOR SUBSEQUENT FREE-MARKET ECONOMISTS TO BUILD UPON ULTIMATELY ORESME BELIEVED THAT THE PRODUCTION OF MONEY SHOULD BE LEFT TO THE FREE MARKET.

05 THE MEDICI FAMILY

C.1397–1737

No family has contributed more to the development of medieval banking than the Medici.

Established in c.1397 and based in Florence, at their height in the 15th century the Medici family operated the largest bank in Europe, and were Europe's wealthiest family. With their great wealth came great power; the Medici's rose to become highly influential in Italy and later throughout Europe. The family produced four Popes and two regent Queens of France.

So respected was the 'Medici Bank' that they acted as private bankers for most European royalty and nobility, and at one point the currency issued by their bank was accepted tender throughout mainland Europe. In 1413 Giovanni di Bicci de'Medici was appointed banker to the Pope.

With their great wealth, the Medici family became the single biggest sponsor of art and architecture in history, mainly early and High Renaissance. Michelangelo, Donatello, Fra Angelico, Leonardo Da Vinci and Raphael were all funded by the Medici family during their careers.

However, as the bank expanded throughout Europe, the Medici Bank found many of its high net-worth clients to often prove unreliable. Their London bank, for example, was forced to shut in 1478 following its loans to Edward IV who became unable to repay his loans following the Wars of the Roses.

After a series of mismanagements by successive Medici heirs, the eventual fall of the Medici Bank came in the late 15th century, when the Medici family's fiscal problems became so severe that they began raiding Florence's state treasuries, at one point defrauding the 'Monte delle Dote', a national charitable fund.

The 1494 invasion of Italy led by King Charles VIII of France caused the eventual collapse of the bank, at which point the bank's remaining assets were seized and all branches were declared dissolved.

THE FAMOUS SCIENTIST GALILEO TUTORED THE MEDICI CHILDREN, AND HE NAMED THE FOUR MOONS OF JUPITER AFTER FOUR OF THE MEDICI CHILDREN.

THE MEDICI'S WERE TRUE RENAISSANCE INNOVATORS. IN ADDITION TO THE PLETHORA OF RENAISSANCE ART AND ARCHITECTURE THEY SPONSORED, SOME OF THE FAMILY'S GREATEST CONTRIBUTIONS INCLUDED THE DEVELOPMENT OF DOUBLE ENTRY BOOKKEEPING TO RECORD FINANCIAL TRANSACTIONS AND THE PIANO.

06 JOHN LAW

1671–1729

On an early spring morning in 1694, screams rang out through London's Bloomsbury Square. A young man fell to the ground, murdered in a duel over a love interest. The killer, a Scottish man with a penchant for gambling, was sentenced to prison. Subsequently escaping, the young man fled to Amsterdam. The man's name was John Law.

Law travelled around Europe for ten years, initially gambling, but later studying international finance. During this time, Law climbed the ranks of European finance, playing roles in various financial speculations and eventually surfacing as the Controller General of Finances for France. With the French economy in ruins from many lengthy and expensive wars, Law quickly set about to prove himself. Within two years he had increased French industry by 60% and lifted French export shipping activities from 16 to a fleet of over 300.

In August 1717, Law became Chief Director of the 'Compagnie d'Occident' (or, the 'Mississippi Company'); a joint stock company owning the French monopoly rights for the exclusive exploration and trade of French colonies in the West Indies and North America.

In an early example of market manipulation, a hugely exaggerated report was presented back in Paris on the prospects of the company's explorations, leading to rampant speculation in the shares, causing a classic stock market feedback loop (the stock price rose from 500 to 10,000 livre).

By 1720, as both Controller General of French Finances and the head of France's most successful public company, Law quickly became one of France's wealthiest and most influential men.

The popularity of Law's Mississippi Company shares was so great that they fuelled demand for more paper bank notes. However, Law's position left him faced with a gigantic conflict of interest; should he continue to print more money to drive up the share price of his own company? In effect, Law was running a Ponzi scheme but on a national level.

The music stopped at the end of 1720, when rumours began circulating in Paris of the true condition of the Louisiana lands. They were far from the fertile, rich and prosperous utopia that Law's marketing campaign had promised. Fearing the worst, investors scrambled to sell their shares, causing the Mississippi share price to plummet; bursting the first ever stock market bubble. Street riots and widespread pandemonium ensued, resulting in Law having to flee yet another country. The event nudged France's fiscal situation one step closer towards its eventual revolution.

Following the events of the Mississippi bubble, Law had no money and very few friends. In a sad twist of irony, Law returned to the very activity he started doing all those years ago; gambling. Aged 57 and impoverished, on 21st March 1729 Law died of pneumonia in Venice.

"L'ECONOMIE, C'EST MOI!"

JOHN LAW ("I AM THE ECONOMY") FROM
PHILOSOPHY, POLITICS AND ECONOMICS

07 SIR JOHN BLUNT

1665–1733

Sir John Blunt, one of the world's most notorious Chairmen, created what has become known as one of history's most extreme cases of stock market speculation, manipulation, boom and bust.

Founded in 1711, the South Sea Company was established with the noble intention of creating a successful, state-sponsored foreign trading company, the profits of which would be used to stabilize Britain's public debt problems and to pay back debts on the British Army and Navy.

As chairman, Blunt purposefully ran the company with a degree of mystery; the more confusion, he believed, the better. By donating shares to a variety of prominent statesmen and society figures (including King George I), Blunt was able to align the financial interests of the establishment with that of the company, in addition to elevating the status of the company with the public. The fact that even the King was a shareholder made the public even more confident that it was a 'safe bet'.

Blunt spread rumours about the 'spectacular potential' that the company had found during its trade in the New World, announcing that the company would grow to be like nothing the world had ever seen. In the spring of 1720, the share price of the South Sea Company rocketed skywards with Blunt doing everything he could to further manipulate the price. The company even offered loans to prospective shareholders, financed simply by new share issues.

In 1720, Blunt announced that a 'midsummer dividend' of a generous 10% would be paid (of course, Blunt secretly bought call options on the midsummer dividend before the announcement ...). By the end of the year, the company not only announced a 30% dividend, but guaranteed a 50% dividend for the next 12 years.

Many investors were going from rags to riches almost overnight, and by the end of 1720 the share price had reached a staggering £1,000 (having been £130 only five months earlier), at which point many of the largest shareholders decided to cash out. As a result of the sell-off the share price plummeted 80% in four weeks. Even as it collapsed, out of desperation Blunt made large support purchases to try to steady the collapsing share price.

The crash left thousands of investors bankrupt; hundreds of them even committed suicide.

Following the crash, Blunt and the other board members were sentenced to the Tower of London, with hundreds of millions of pounds (in today's money) being confiscated from them. The ensuing court case revealed that in some cases bribes of up to £40 million (in today's money) were paid to government officials.

Thomas Guy, a successful investor in the South Sea Bubble, felt guilty about being one of few who profited (legally) from the scheme. He used part of his fortune to build 'Guy's Hospital', still one of the largest in London.

The South Sea Company story is often cited as one of the greatest examples of a stock market bubble. The 'greater fool' investment strategy (where speculators deliberately buy stocks in the hope that a 'greater fool' will pay even more for them before the bubble bursts) was a driving force in the price of the South Sea Company's stock. Today many call it 'momentum investing', that is, rapidly adapting to changing circumstances in the stock markets to 'ride the wave' to profit.

"I CAN CALCULATE THE MOVEMENT OF THE STARS BUT NOT THE MADNESS OF MEN!"

SIR ISAAC NEWTON, WHO LOST APPROXIMATELY £3 MILLION IN TODAY'S MONEY IN THE SOUTH SEA COMPANY

08 ADAM SMITH

1723–1790

The Wealth of Nations stands in history as one of the most influential books ever written. Later to become known as the 'godfather of economics', essentially Adam Smith's ideas on the role of society, government, trade and enterprise have facilitated the functionality of our society ever since.

Before Smith, people believed that a nation's wealth could be judged simply by its stocks of gold and silver. 'Importing' was seen as harmful to a nation (because it resulted in an outflow of this wealth), whilst exporting, the reverse, was viewed favourably. As a result, nations adopted extensive protectionist policies; large subsidies for exporters set-off against large tariffs on imports.

Smith transformed this concept by showing that measuring a nation's wealth is not as simple as the sum of its gold and silver reserves, but the total stream of all its goods and services (what we now call 'aggregate demand'). How does a nation maximize this stream? Easily, Smith argued; set it free.

Radical thinking at the time, Smith brought a fresh approach to the understanding of human behaviour within society showing how free, open trade yields the most efficient model of resource allocation. In a free exchange, both sides can become better off; after all, nobody would trade if they expected to lose from it. Smith explained that it is therefore human nature, not governments and ministers, which will ultimately provide the competitive, receptive environment within which an economy will flourish. And it is the poor that will benefit the most from this state of economic and social freedom.

Wouldn't our greedy, self-interested human nature cause mayhem if we were all let loose within a free market? Not according to Smith, who outlined that when individuals can choose freely what to produce and what to purchase, the market's 'invisible hand' will guide society. A state of social harmony will emerge naturally as human beings struggle to find ways to live and work with each other. Does a baker make bread out of an altruistic desire to quell our hunger? Of course not. They sell bread because they want to make money – and it is this individual pursuit of 'greed' that drives an economy forward; the 'invisible hand' transforming individual greed into the greater good of collective gain.

Smith's ideas greatly influenced his contemporary politicians, laying the foundations for the great 19th century era of free trade and economic expansion.

We mustn't think of Smith as purely an economist; his work provides a groundbreaking presentation of the rich and varied composition of ethics, psychology, morality and welfare to offer an understanding of how, and why, we behave as we do within society.

"IT IS NOT FROM THE BENEVOLENCE OF THE BUTCHER, THE BREWER, OR THE BAKER THAT WE EXPECT OUR DINNER, BUT FROM THEIR REGARD TO THEIR OWN SELF-INTEREST."

ADAM SMITH FROM *THE WEALTH OF NATIONS*

09 CHARLES HALL

1740–1825

Can buying luxury goods make someone else poorer? What do we actually mean by 'wealth'?

The 19th century doctor-turned-economist Dr Charles Hall is widely regarded as the forerunner of the modern socialist movement.

Educated in the Netherlands, it was when practising medicine in rural Devon that Hall was exposed to the many food shortages and sub-standard living conditions of the working classes of the time. In particular, Hall was concerned with how the Industrial Revolution, whilst enormously increasing the country's productive capacity, had affected the living conditions of the working classes.

Whilst disagreeing with a large amount of their ideas, Hall closely studied the works of contemporary classical economists such as Adam Smith, Thomas Malthus and David Ricardo. Reflecting upon their ideas, in 1805 Hall subsequently synthesized his economic theories and personal critiques of capitalism in his landmark book *The Effects of Civilization on the People in European States*.

In his book, Hall proposed that "wealth consists not in things but in power over the labour of others". In essence, Hall believed that society's problems emanated from the ability of the wealthy to determine what is produced, through their control of others. The masses grow poorer from 'civilization' in a process whereby the increase in wealth at the top is only made possible by the increase in poverty at the bottom.

Hall's explanation for this centred upon his 'surplus argument', which highlights that the wealthy, unlike the poor, are able to not only afford their own basic essentials but also to have a surplus left over. This surplus duly gets spent on what Hall deems as 'luxuries', and it is this spending which "make[s] it possible for a rich man to consume and destroy infinitely more of the produce of other men's labours than he would be able to do if only foodstuffs and basic necessities were available".

Put simply, Hall argued that the increasing power of the rich causes the suffering of the poor; "the wealth of the rich and the misery of the poor increase in strict proportions".

To solve this, Hall proposed several remedies such as progressive taxation, prohibiting marriage between two landowners (i.e. wealthy people) and prohibiting or heavily taxing luxury goods.

As a pioneer, Hall's works were a catalyst for the plethora of socialist and Marxist thought that was to follow.

"...A TRUE PHENOMENON IN THE HISTORY OF ECONOMIC THOUGHT."

KARL MARX DESCRIBING HALL

10 THE ROTHSCHILD FAMILY
C.1744—PRESENT DAY

The Rothschild family stands as possibly the most well known banking dynasty in modern history. With origins dating back to the late 18th century, to this day the notoriously discreet Rothschild family have stood as key players in international high finance, amassing one of the largest private fortunes in the process.

The rise of the family's empire began in 1744, when Mayer Amschel Rothschild created his finance house, spreading his empire by placing each of his five sons in different European cities.

Largely in response to the racial and politically-motivated violence that existed in 18th century Germany towards Jews, the family pioneered the development of financial instruments such as stocks, bonds and debt, thus making their wealth beyond the reaches of rioters and distrusting monarchs.

AS THE MAJOR LENDER TO MOST EUROPEAN GOVERNMENTS, THE ROTHSCHILDS BECAME SO POWERFUL THAT MANY BELIEVED THEM TO BE INDIRECTLY CONTROLLING MOST OF WESTERN EUROPE. WARS WERE WON AND LOST DEPENDING UPON WHICH SIDE THE ROTHSCHILDS SUPPORTED. MANY BELIEVE THAT THE OUTCOME OF THE NAPOLEONIC WARS WAS ESSENTIALLY DECIDED WHEN THE ROTHSCHILDS DECIDED TO PUT THEIR FINANCIAL WEIGHT BEHIND BRITAIN.

The network of agents and couriers that the family had established allowed them to transport large amounts of gold quickly and safely throughout Europe. The network also provided a reliable, rapid source of financial and political information, giving the family a significant knowledge advantage in the financial markets and making them invaluable to governments. Legend speculates that Nathan, the brother in London, reportedly received news of Wellington's victory at the Battle of Waterloo 24 hours before the British government did.

Companies that have been founded or financed by the Rothschilds include Rio Tinto, DeBeers and the Suez Canal. Today, the family still enjoys great prominence in the global banking and political industry. Famous for their philanthropy, it is widely reported that a significant proportion of the art in the world's top art galleries has been 'anonymously donated' by the family over the years.

FOR MOST OF THE 20TH CENTURY THE PRICE OF GOLD WAS FIXED TWICE A DAY AT THE LONDON PREMISES OF N M ROTHSCHILD BY MEMBERS OF THE LONDON GOLD MARKET FIXING

11 DAVID RICARDO

1772–1823

The third of 17 children born to a Sephardic Jewish immigrant family, David Ricardo began his adult life working with his father as a stock broker in London.

Aged 21 Ricardo fell in love with a Quaker, upon which he turned his back on Judaism. Subsequently thrown out of the family Ricardo started his own stockbrokers which, proving successful, allowed him to retire comfortably aged 42.

However, it was whilst holidaying in Bath in 1799 that Ricardo read a book that was to change his life forever. It was called *The Wealth of Nations*, the author, Adam Smith. It was Ricardo's first significant contact with the world of economics, and immediately he was hooked. Ricardo spent the rest of his life as a professional economist. He became an MP, and befriended many of the celebrated thinkers of the day such as Thomas Malthus and James Mills.

As an early advocate of monetary policy, Ricardo was first recognized amongst economists in 1809 when, during the 'bullion controversy', he (controversially) wrote that England's inflation was as a result of the Bank of England printing too many bank notes.

Perhaps Ricardo's greatest achievement was his development of what we now know as 'diminishing marginal returns', in which Ricardo showed that if one factor of production (e.g. number of workers) is increased whilst other factors (e.g. workspace, machines) are held constant, then the additions to output per unit of the variable factor (workers) will eventually diminish. Proof that too many cooks (will eventually) spoil the broth!

Through his opposition to the protectionist Corn Laws, Ricardo passionately argued in favour of free trade, and in doing so formulated the key economic theory of comparative advantage; arguing that if a country can get products from abroad at a lower cost than it could make them itself, then it will make them better off to do so. Through 'comparative advantage' Ricardo advocated in favour of industry specialism and free trade.

Rent theory (the difference between the raw costs of production and the price) is the third of Ricardo's great economic contributions; 'Ricardian Rents' was the first clear explanation of the source and magnitude of land rents, outlining that multiple grades of land are needed in order for 'rent' to exist.

"GOLD...THOUGH OF LITTLE USE COMPARED WITH AIR OR WATER, WILL EXCHANGE FOR A GREAT QUANTITY OF OTHER GOODS."

DAVID RICARDO FROM PRINCIPLES OF POLITICAL ECONOMY AND TAXATION

12 KARL MARX

1818–1883

The philosopher, social scientist and revolutionary Karl Marx, was undoubtedly the 19th century's most influential figure in socialist thought and played a key role in the cultivation of socialism, and the development of communism. His theories on politics, society, religion and economics have collectively become known as 'Marxism'. Largely ignored during his lifetime, his ideas were adopted and disseminated by the socialist movement after his death.

Marx criticized the existing socio-economic structure, calling capitalism the 'dictatorship of the bourgeoisie'. Marx believed that the capitalist system produces internal tensions which will inevitably lead to self-destruction, at which point socialism will rise up in its place. In time, this state of socialism, Marx argued, will be replaced by a stateless, classless society which he termed 'pure communism'. Calling upon the working classes, Marx actively encouraged revolutionary action against capitalism.

Born into a wealthy middle class Jewish family in Prussia, Marx became a journalist in Cologne before moving to Paris in 1843. During his transition to become a revolutionary communist, he met his life-long associate Friedrich Engels. Exiled from France in 1845, Marx moved to Brussels, where he became an active figure in the 'Communist League'. In 1848 Marx and Engels co-authored *The Communist Manifesto*; outlining that all human history has been based upon class struggles, predicting the end of capitalism. Acting as the fundamental charter of most (if not all) communist states to rise and fall in the past 100 years, Marx's manifesto has acted as the primary catalyst for communism.

The following year Marx moved to London. Much of Marx's most prolific piece, *Das Kapital*, (which many now refer to as the 'Bible of the working class') put forward his theories of how all profits result from an 'exploitation of labour'.

"THE THEORY OF COMMUNISTS MAY BE SUMMED UP IN THE SINGLE SENTENCE: ABOLITION OF PRIVATE PROPERTY."

KARL MARX FROM THE COMMUNIST MANIFESTO

"LET THE RULING CLASSES TREMBLE AT A COMMUNISTIC REVOLUTION. THE PROLETARIANS HAVE NOTHING TO LOSE BUT THEIR CHAINS. THEY HAVE A WORLD TO WIN.

WORKING MEN OF ALL COUNTRIES, UNITE!"

KARL MARX FROM THE COMMUNIST MANIFESTO

13 VILFREDO PARETO

1848–1923

Why are some people wealthy whilst most are not? How is wealth distributed? How and why do the 'rich' remain so for generations? To answer these questions, we turn to Vilfredo Pareto.

Born into exiled Genoese nobility in 1848, Pareto was one of the first economists to convincingly apply statistical modelling to the many problems of economics.

Captivated by ideas of power and wealth, Pareto analysed vast quantities of tax, income and property records throughout Europe, plotting his results graphically. Startlingly, in different countries, throughout different eras, the same conclusions were consistently reached; the majority of people sit at the bottom of society, whilst only a small handful of the elite ruling class sit at the top. Nor, Pareto added, did this occur by chance.

The 'Pareto Principle', named after his studies of Italian land ownership, highlights that in many cases, roughly 80% of the effects come from 20% of the causes. Sounds silly, right? Not necessarily... throughout numerous real-world cases, the idea of 80% of the power (or wealth) being concentrated with (or attributed to) 20% of the population does indeed hold true.

Almost Darwinian in perspective, Pareto believed in the futileness of democracy, where the intelligent, stronger members of society thrive at the expense of the weaker, less intelligent.

Still today, the 'Pareto Principle' can be seen in a number of different scenarios, for example it is common to find that 80% of a company's profits come from 20% of their customer base, or alternatively 80% of crime is committed by 20% of criminals.

Interestingly, in 2002 Microsoft noted that by fixing the top 20% of the most reported bugs, 80% of error reports are eliminated.

IN SHORT, PARETO PIONEERED MICROECONOMICS; CHANNELLING ECONOMICS FROM THE SERIES OF MORAL QUESTIONINGS SIMILAR IN STRUCTURE TO ADAM SMITH'S WORKS, INTO THE STATISTICAL AND EMPIRICALLY DEMANDING SCIENTIFIC FIELD OF RESEARCH THAT WE LIVE IN TODAY.

'PARETO EFFICIENCY' IS THE TERM USED TO DESCRIBE THE STATE THAT OCCURS WHEN NO ONE CAN BE MADE BETTER OFF WITHOUT SOMEONE ELSE BEING MADE WORSE OFF.

14 AMADEO P. GIANNINI

1870–1949

One hundred years ago a regular person could not simply walk into a bank and open an account; current accounts, mortgages and loans were very much the preserve of the rich. Amadeo P. Giannini changed all of that, transforming modern international banking and creating the largest bank in the country (at that time) in the process.

Following a successful career in the Californian produce industry, Giannini became a banker at the age of 34, more by accident than by design when the death of Giannini's father-in-law forced him to take up his position on the board of a small bank in San Francisco.

At the bank, Giannini was frustrated at how the bank would only lend to wealthy clients. Enduring countless arguments with the other directors he fought desperately to convince the company that lending to the working classes was not only morally right, but could also be immensely profitable. His experience as the son of Italian immigrants taught him how hard-working and trustworthy the working and middle classes could be.

GIANNINI FINANCED THE CONSTRUCTION OF THE GOLDEN GATE BRIDGE.

Unsuccessful in his pleas, Giannini branched out on his own, opening his own bank in 1904. From the outset, Giannini was determined to 'fight for the little people', routinely lending money to farmers and labourers and encouraging poor immigrants to deposit money with him rather than keeping it as cash.

In the wake of the 1906 San Francisco earthquake, realizing the desperation of many of the city's working classes who's homes and businesses had been destroyed, Giannini went down to the beachfront and set up shop by placing a plank of wood over two barrels, firm in the belief that San Francisco would rise from the ashes. From here Giannini began to lend money to small businesses and individuals desperately in need, receiving only a handshake as his guarantee in some cases.

His actions that day made him a local hero and were to change his life forever. He realized the life-changing power that banking could provide to the ordinary man. From that day forward, he was determined to develop his bank into a nationwide system of branches, bringing money and financial services to everyone, regardless of their wealth.

By the time of his death, Giannini's 'Bank of America' was the largest bank in the USA, and the largest privately held bank in the world. After his death, much of his fortune was left to a foundation for medical research.

DESPITE HIS HUGE SUCCESS, GIANNINI NEVER TOOK MUCH MONEY OUT OF HIS BUSINESS FOR HIMSELF. THIS LED TO HIS NICKNAME 'THE RELUCTANT MILLIONAIRE'; HE WAS NEVER REALLY IN IT FOR THE MONEY.

IN ITS INFANCY THE MOVIE INDUSTRY WAS SEEN AS HIGH RISK, AND POTENTIALLY JUST A CRAZE. GIANNINI SAW PAST THIS, FUNDING AMONGST OTHERS MANY *CHARLIE CHAPLIN FILMS*, *WEST SIDE STORY*, *LAWRENCE OF ARABIA*, *GONE WITH THE WIND* AND THE MAJORITY OF WALT DISNEY'S EARLY MOVIES.

15 CHARLES PONZI

1882–1949

On 15th November 1903, a 21 year old slick talking Italian man stepped off the SS Vancouver at Boston Harbour with '$2.50 in cash and $1 million in hopes'. The man was Charles Ponzi, and he was to deliver a financial scam with such flair and confidence, that it would elevate him to the ranks of the greatest fraudsters of all time.

Ponzi's scheme centred on a weakness in the 'International Postal Reply Coupons' system. The idea of the postal reply coupons was to cover postal charges for a reply to a letter from abroad. Since IRCs were valued in the country of purchase, yet exchanged for stamps in the country where redeemed, the price difference, if any, provided an opportunity for arbitrage.

High inflation after World War 1 reduced the cost of postage in Italy, the result being that an IRC could be bought cheaply in Italy and exchanged for US stamps with a higher value, which could subsequently be sold for a profit.

Ponzi established the 'Securities Exchange Company', promising investors a 50% return within 45 days. Within weeks, Ponzi was the new hotshot money manager in town. Queues formed outside his offices with thousands of people wanting to purchase Ponzi promissory notes, with many

> **WITHIN FOUR MONTHS PONZI'S COMPANY HAD EARNED HIM OVER £100 MILLION IN TODAY'S MONEY**

remortgaging their homes to do so. Ponzi became a millionaire within a few months, and at his peak, in 1920, he was making $250,000 per day. So arrogant was Ponzi, that when a local journalist suggested his rates of return to be dubious, Ponzi had the arrogance to sue for libel, winning $500,000 in damages.

Of course, there were no actual profits; Ponzi didn't even buy the IRCs – he was simply using new investor money to repay old investors, whilst taking a substantial cut for himself.

In the summer of 1920, a journalist pointed out that to cover the investments that Ponzi was purportedly making, 160 million IRC coupons would have to be in circulation. The real number stood at a mere 27,000.

The genie was out of the bottle. With investors queuing down the street to withdraw their money, on 12th August 1920, Ponzi surrendered himself to the federal authorities.

"I WENT LOOKING FOR TROUBLE AND I FOUND IT" WERE PONZI'S LAST WORDS ON AMERICAN SOIL, AS HE WAS DEPORTED BACK TO ITALY FOLLOWING HIS 12 YEAR JAIL SENTENCE.

"...I HAD GIVEN THEM THE BEST SHOW THAT WAS EVER STAGED IN THEIR TERRITORY SINCE THE LANDING OF THE PILGRIMS!"

PONZI IN HIS FINAL INTERVIEW BEFORE HIS DEATH

16 ALVES DOS REIS

1898–1955

Alves dos Reis stands as one of the most notorious figures in the history of money.

Armed with a forged diploma from Oxford University, Reis spent the early part of his career amassing a fortune by buying a stake in the Transafrican Railways of Angola (using an uncovered cheque), and by buying a US car dealership (forging cheques to buy it, and then covering it by using the money in the firm's reserves).

However, Reis' defining moment came in 1924, when he conceived his masterplan; he was to attempt to hijack the entire money supply of the Banco de Portugal.

He began by forging a contract for the production of Portuguese legal tender in the bank's name. Reis informed the printers that the notes were for a large, unannounced development loan to Angola (and as such for political reasons had to be treated in complete confidentiality). Reis assured the printers that they would stamp the word 'ANGOLA' onto the new notes, and hence they could simply be printed with the serial numbers similar to the banknotes already circulating in Portugal. Hence Reis figured, with the printers accepting the forged documentation in confidentiality, and with the actual banknotes technically being legal, the plan would be undetectable.

REIS' FLAMBOYANT HOUSE, THE 'PALACE OF THE GOLDEN BOY', IS NOW THE BUILDING OF THE BRITISH COUNCIL IN LISBON.

Reis' printers produced 100 million escudos, representing approximately 1% of Portugal's GDP at the time. Within a year, Reis had introduced banknotes worth over £1 billion into the Portuguese economy. Reis laundered the notes into circulation through the creation of the 'Bank of Angola and Metropole'.

Initially, the plan worked perfectly as whilst there were rumours of fake banknotes in circulation, Reis' notes were technically not counterfeited as such (just produced without authorization). Unfortunately for Reis, his newly-formed bank increasingly attracted the attention of local journalists, who soon realized that it was offering low interest loans without the need for receiving deposits. On 5th December 1925, Reis' fraud was publicly revealed by the Portuguese flagship newspaper, *O Século*.

The revelation of the fraud had dramatic repercussions on the Portuguese economy. The exchange rate of the Portuguese escudo fell, and a crisis of confidence in the Portuguese government followed. More sinisterly, the fraud was said to have had a huge influence on the public's emotions, which brought about the 1926 nationalist military coup, resulting in the *Ditadura Nacional* (national dictatorship) of Prime Minister António de Oliveira Salazar from 1932 to 1968.

In May 1930, Reis (then aged 32) was tried for masterminding the fraud, being convicted and duly sentenced to 20 years in prison.

DURING HIS TRIAL, REIS' FORGED
DOCUMENTS WERE SO CONVINCING
THAT IT DELAYED THE SENTENCE
FOR ALMOST FIVE YEARS
WHILST THE PORTUGUESE COURTS
TRIED TO ESTABLISH WHAT WAS
REAL AND WHAT WAS FAKE.

17 J.P. MORGAN

1837–1913

The leading financier of the 'Progressive Era', John Pierpont Morgan was an American Industrialist, banker and corporate visionary famous for preventing the 1907 US banking crisis, and accredited with the founding of the J.P. Morgan empire.

Morgan dominated the US corporate landscape; playing pivotal roles in the merging, underwriting, reorganization and consolidations of the majority of the deals that dominated the period. In reference to his effectiveness at corporate reorganization, 'Morganization' became a common industry reference.

With a strong commitment to culture and religion, Morgan's visionary passion for efficiency, business modernization and economies of scale helped to revolutionize American corporatism, initiating the wave of corporate consolidation that dominated the early 20th century.

Following the 'Interstate Commerce Act' in 1887, it was Morgan who brought together railroad executives to synthesize the implementations of the new laws. When the Federal Treasury was running out of gold in 1895, it was Morgan who created a private syndicate on Wall Street to save the Treasury by supplying it with gold to finance a bond issue.

And when the 'Panic of 1907' threatened to cripple the American economy, it was Morgan who took charge; inviting America's leading financiers to his New York mansion to devise the plan that redirected and channelled money to pump life into the US financial system.

Put simply, Morgan was influential in almost every part of corporate America; from the railroads to *The New York Times* from Carnegie Steel to General Electric. In fact, Morgan's extensive influence on both Wall Street and in public planning led to accusations of him indirectly controlling the nation's high finances.

"NEVER SELL AMERICA SHORT."

J.P. MORGAN FROM THE PROTESTANT ESTABLISHMENT

"A MAN ALWAYS HAS TWO REASONS FOR DOING ANYTHING: A GOOD REASON AND THE REAL REASON."

J.P. MORGAN FROM ROOSEVELT:
THE STORY OF A FRIENDSHIP

"THE FIRST STEP TOWARDS GETTING SOMEWHERE IS TO DECIDE THAT YOU ARE NOT GOING TO STAY WHERE YOU ARE."

J.P. MORGAN FROM COURAGE FOR THE JOURNEY

"IF YOU HAVE TO ASK THE PRICE, THEN YOU PROBABLY CAN'T AFFORD IT."

J.P. MORGAN ON OWNING A YACHT

18 FRANKLIN D. ROOSEVELT

1882–1945

"So, first of all, let me assert my firm belief that the only thing we have to fear...is fear itself" began Franklin D. Roosevelt's inauguration speech in 1933.

The 'fear' he was referring to, of course, was the 25% US unemployment rate, the 50% drop in US GDP and the 32 states that had closed their banks. In the wake of the 1929 Wall Street Crash, capitalism, it would seem, was doomed.

At the time of Roosevelt's inauguration, the US economy (and in many ways modern capitalism itself) was at a crossroads. Following the 1929 Wall Street Crash, the US was experiencing the Great Depression, with a vast wave of economic, political and cultural reforms becoming increasingly essential.

Tackling the situation head-on, through his 'New Deal' programme Roosevelt initiated a vital, wide-ranging series of major social reforms to the US economy.

Essentially, the New Deal was centred on the 3 R's; relief, recovery and reform. The New Deal provided reforms to almost all aspects of US society, from the introduction of social security payments to the repeal of prohibition.

To boost confidence and stimulate activity in the banking sector, the New Deal was responsible for the creation of the Glass-Steagall Act of 1933 (providing a firewall between investment and retail banking), Federal Deposit Insurance Corporation (providing a government guarantee for bank deposits) and the creation of the Securities and Exchange Commission.

Roosevelt sought not to contest the system of private profit, but to regulate and channel it. As a result, Roosevelt's New Deal unquestionably accelerated the recovery of the US economy from the Great Depression. In sum, Roosevelt's New Deal saved capitalism and the principles of privately owned business for the US economy.

ROOSEVELT'S PROGRAMS "RESTED ON THE ASSUMPTION THAT A JUST SOCIETY COULD BE SECURED BY IMPOSING A WELFARE STATE ON A CAPITALIST FOUNDATION."

HISTORIAN WILLIAM E. LEUCHTENBURG FROM FRANKLIN D. ROOSEVELT AND THE NEW DEAL

IN 1921 ROOSEVELT SUDDENLY FELL ILL WITH POLIO, WHICH LEFT HIM UNABLE TO WALK AND IN A WHEELCHAIR.

WHILST DOCTORS ADVISED HIM THAT HIS POLITICAL CAREER WAS OVER, THROUGH THE SUPPORT OF HIS WIFE (ELEANOR) WHO ACTED AS HIS SUBSTITUTE IN MEETINGS WHEN REQUIRED, AND THROUGH SHEER DETERMINATION ROOSEVELT TAUGHT HIMSELF TO WALK AGAIN USING BRACES AND A CANE.

19 WADDILL CATCHINGS

1879–1967

When you hear the name 'Goldman Sachs' what do you think of? Top tier, elite investment bank? Less well known, however, is that one man came very close to bankrupting the bank during the stock market crash of 1929...

...In the late 1920s, a 'closed fund mania' was sweeping through Wall Street – everybody was getting involved, and funds were trading with large premiums over Net Asset Values (NAV). Goldman Sachs was the largest player in the closed-end fund market; "well, the people want them" reportedly spoke a Goldman Sachs partner when asked why they had formed so many.

Goldman Sachs employee Waddill Catchings, a leading banker at the time, devised an innovative structure with which the bank could amplify its trading profits. Catchings thus convinced the bank to open a closed-end fund, naming it the Goldman Sachs Trading Corporation (GSTC).

In the summer of 1929, it launched the Shenandoah Corporation, a trust with GSTC holding most of the common stock, and selling the remaining common stock and preferred stock to the public. In essence, this created a fund of funds with leverage. In turn, the Shenandoah Corporation then set up the Blue Ridge Corporation, retaining most of the common stock itself, and selling the remaining common and preferred stock to the public. This now created a fund of funds with leverage at two levels; any gain in Blue Ridge would be transmitted to Shenandoah with leverage, which in turn would be further augmented as they flowed back into Goldman Sachs.

The funds performed well at first, with Catchings initially being hailed as a financial genius...

...but what everyone had failed to consider was that essentially all that Catchings had created for Goldman Sachs was a hugely leveraged, exposed position. Admittedly, if stock prices rose, then the profit, leveraged at two levels, would be large. But what if stock prices fell? The magnification process would still happen, but it would flow the other way.

In the crash of 1929, Catching found out the hard way; causing the GSTC stock to plummet from a high of $280 to $1.25 per share in 1932. The fund very nearly bankrupted Goldman Sachs, and damaged its reputation for many years afterwards.

"IT IS DIFFICULT NOT TO MARVEL AT THE IMAGINATION WHICH WAS IMPLICIT IN THIS GARGANTUAN INSANITY."

JOHN KENNETH GALBRAITH FROM THE GREAT CRASH 1929

20 HETTY GREEN

1834–1916

Hetty Green, aka the 'Witch of Wall Street', was an American businesswoman, and the first female tycoon to make a significant impact in the world of finance.

Born into a wealthy Quaker family in Massachusetts, by the age of six Green was reading the financial press daily and by the age of 13 she became the family bookkeeper.

Green's investment strategy was simple; conservative buying backed by substantial cash reserves to cover any movements in her positions. Over her career, Green amassed a fortune of approximately $200 million (about $4 billion in today's money), making her the world's richest woman at the time.

In one of the earliest modern examples of a pre-nuptial agreement, in 1867 Green made her fiancé sign a document renouncing all rights to her money before their marriage. Following their marriage, Green and her husband emigrated to London, taking up residence at the Langham Hotel.

Was she deserving of her nickname the Witch of Wall Street? Perhaps not, however, she was certainly a miser. Despite her amassed fortune Green reportedly refused to use hot water or heating, and chose to wear only one black dress, which she would not change unless it was worn out. Allegedly her laundress was instructed to only wash the obviously dirty parts of her clothes, so as to avoid wasting soap. Her diet consisted of cheap pies and oatmeal, which she heated on the office radiator.

When her son, Ned, broke his leg, Green tried to admit him to a free clinic for the poor, before being recognized and reluctantly being forced to pay the medical bill. In her later life, Green often moved between small apartments, so as to avoid attracting the attention of local tax officials. In her last years, Green developed a hernia but refused to treat it due to the $150 cost.

Green died aged 81 in New York City, leaving one of the largest inheritance packages in the history of the USA to her two children.

WHEN LEARNING THAT HER AUNT HAD GIVEN ALMOST $2 MILLION TO CHARITY IN HER WILL, GREEN DISPUTED ITS VALIDITY, PRODUCING IN COURT AN EARLIER VERSION IN WHICH THE ENTIRE ESTATE WAS TO BE LEFT TO GREEN. GREEN LOST THE CASE WHEN THE COURT CONCLUDED THAT GREEN'S EVIDENCE HAD BEEN FORGED.

"THERE IS NO GREAT SECRET IN FORTUNE-MAKING. ALL YOU DO IS BUY CHEAP AND SELL DEAR, ACT WITH THRIFT AND SHREWDNESS AND BE PERSISTENT."

HETTY GREEN, NATIONAL MAGAZINE, 1905

21 F.A. HAYEK

1899–1992

The Austrian economist Friedrich A. Hayek was the leading libertarian social theorist of the 20th century. Best known for his defence of classical liberalism and free-market capitalism against socialism, Hayek's works provide a groundbreaking account of what he believed were the misguided assumptions of social planning.

Whilst serving in World War 1, Hayek witnessed first-hand what he considered to be the destructiveness of a socialist regime. Determined to change the socialist attitudes that he believed led to the war, after the conflict Hayek pursued a career in academia. As a result the global Great Depression and the rising interest in Nazi fascism served as a significant platform upon which Hayek formulated his theories.

Hayek argued that despite the temptation of socialist ideas, in reality they can only be accomplished by means that few would approve of. Addressing fascism and socialism, he reveals that oppression and tyranny are ultimately the only products that such ideas will harvest. Hayek believed that socialism has, from its conception, been based upon mistaken ideals.

> "A SOCIETY THAT DOES NOT RECOGNIZE THAT EACH INDIVIDUAL HAS VALUES OF HIS OWN WHICH HE IS ENTITLED TO FOLLOW CAN HAVE NO RESPECT FOR THE DIGNITY OF THE INDIVIDUAL AND CANNOT REALLY KNOW FREEDOM."
>
> *F.A. HAYEK FROM THE MARKET*

Referring to it as the 'fatal conceit', Hayek believed that the fundamental problem with socialism is the misguided belief that man is able to successfully shape the world around him.

A staunch believer in the 'Economic Calculation Problem', Hayek believed that changing prices in a free-market system communicate signals which enable individuals to coordinate their plans. Hayek argued that the lack of freedom in centrally planned economies destroys these price signals and hence governments in centrally planned economies lack sufficient information to determine a successful allocation of resources.

Hayek's *magnum opus* is his 1944 piece *The Road to Serfdom*, which sets out the argument that the abandonment of freedom and individualism in favour of central planning will ultimately lead to fascist oppression. Socialism, he argued, requires central economic planning which in turn leads to totalitarianism.

Another of Hayek's influential works is his 1976 *The Denationalization of Money*, which argues for the development of a free market in money, where money-issuers compete and experiment to discover and produce the most stable, healthy currency. The book harvested the entire free banking movement.

IN THE MIDDLE OF A 1975
CONSERVATIVE RESEARCH
DEPARTMENT LECTURE ON THE
'MIDDLE WAY', MARGARET THATCHER,
THE FAMOUS PRIME MINISTER OF
BRITAIN, REPORTEDLY INTERRUPTED:
SHE STOOD UP, REACHED INTO
HER BRIEFCASE AND REVEALED A
COPY OF HAYEK'S *THE CONSTITUTION
OF LIBERTY* TO THE AUDIENCE. "THIS",
SHE EXCLAIMED, "IS WHAT
WE BELIEVE!"

22 JOHN VON NEUMANN

1903–1957

Von Neumann was born Neumann János Lajos in Budapest in 1903. Considered a child prodigy, by the age of six he was able to memorize telephone directories and could hold a conversation in classical Greek. By eight he was proficient with integral calculus.

Receiving his PhD aged 22 from Budapest's Pázmány Péter University, he emigrated to the United States in 1930, whereupon his name was changed to 'John von Neumann'. Von Neumann accepted a position at Princeton University, where he remained for the rest of his life. As a frequent consultant to the CIA during World War 2, von Neumann played a key role in the development of the first atomic bomb.

Von Neumann is generally regarded as one of the greatest mathematicians in modern history. Throughout his life he wrote 150 published papers, mainly on pure mathematics, applied mathematics and physics. So dedicated to his work was von Neumann, that even whilst on his death bed he wrote his piece *The Computer and the Brain*.

Studying during a period of great worldwide transition, throughout his life von Neumann applied mathematical reasoning in an attempt to model economic situations, with the result being one of the most important contributions to the understanding of economic behaviour; Game Theory. Von

VON NEUMANN SPENT HIS ENTIRE CAREER AT PRINCETON UNIVERSITY, WORKING ALONGSIDE ALBERT EINSTEIN AMONGST OTHERS.

Neumann's revolutionary studies on game theory have allowed us to look at the relationships between participants and predict their optimal decisions.

The 'minimax theorem' published by von Neumann in 1928 was revolutionary in helping economists, governments, financiers and individuals to understand that in a matrix, zero sum game with perfect information, an optimal strategy exists that can result in the minimization of both player's maximum losses.

In 1944, the minimax theorem's application was enhanced to cover the more realistic scenario involving games played with imperfect information and over two players. Called the Theory of Games and Economic Behavior, quite simply it was groundbreaking and attracted worldwide attention. *The New York Times* even ran a front-page story on it.

AN ECCENTRIC INDIVIDUAL, VON NEUMANN REGULARLY HOSTED LEGENDARY PARTIES AT HIS HOME IN PRINCETON. HE WAS A NOTORIOUSLY BAD DRIVER, OFTEN GETTING STOPPED BY THE POLICE FOR TRYING TO READ A BOOK WHILST DRIVING.

VON NEUMANN BELIEVED THAT MUCH OF HIS MATHEMATICAL THOUGHT OCCURRED INTUITIVELY. HE WOULD OFTEN GO TO SLEEP WITH A PROBLEM UNSOLVED, AND KNOW THE ANSWER IMMEDIATELY UPON WAKING.

23 JOSEPH SCHUMPETER
1883–1950

Remember how popular VHS was in the 1990s? Now thanks to DVD and digital, they can't give them away. Remember 35mm camera film? Now everyone's gone digital.

This process, coined by the Austrian-American economist Joseph Schumpeter, is called 'creative destruction' and describes how the old ways of doing things are constantly destroyed and replaced by new, innovative methods. This constant competitive cycle acts as the dynamic current that underlies our economy, propelling our society forward.

Schumpeter argued that in order to survive, companies are forced to consistently improve their designs, efficiencies and innovation rates. If, for example, Boeing didn't have Airbus as a rival, would they face the same incentives to improve their design, service and price? Anyone excited about the release of the next iPhone? Petrified of rival products coming onto the market, Apple Inc will be constantly innovating and developing their new products at the fastest rate they possibly can – ultimately resulting in a better quality iPhone in our pockets. Through this dynamic tension between companies operating in every relatively liberal market throughout our economy, the world around us is constantly being improved and updated; ultimately improving our standard of living.

Schumpeter was a key player in the development of 'evolutionary economics', which emphasizes the critical importance of change; describing economic organizations as dynamic processes experiencing ongoing transformations determined by both individuals and our society.

Schumpeter centred on the understanding of business cycles and development. He saw the Entrepreneur as the hero of the business cycle; disturbing the equilibrium and acting as the prime cause of economic development. He argued that the intellectual and social conditions required to allow entrepreneurship to thrive exist primarily in a capitalist society, with profit being a driving motive.

What would Schumpeter have made of not allowing the banks to fail in the 2008 financial crisis?

"CAPITALISM, THEN, IS BY NATURE A FORM OR METHOD OF ECONOMIC CHANGE AND NOT ONLY NEVER IS BUT NEVER CAN BE STATIONARY... THE FUNDAMENTAL IMPULSE THAT SETS AND KEEPS THE CAPITALIST ENGINE IN MOTION COMES FROM THE NEW CONSUMERS' GOODS, THE NEW METHODS OF PRODUCTION OR TRANSPORTATION, THE NEW MARKETS, THE NEW FORMS OF INDUSTRIAL ORGANIZATION THAT CAPITALIST ENTERPRISE CREATES...

THAT INCESSANTLY REVOLUTIONIZES THE ECONOMIC STRUCTURE *FROM WITHIN,* INCESSANTLY DESTROYING THE OLD ONE, INCESSANTLY CREATING A NEW ONE. THIS PROCESS OF CREATIVE DESTRUCTION IS THE ESSENTIAL FACT ABOUT CAPITALISM. IT IS WHAT CAPITALISM CONSISTS IN AND WHAT EVERY CAPITALIST CONCERN HAS GOT TO LIVE IN."

JOSEPH SCHUMPETER FROM CAPITALISM, SOCIALISM AND DEMOCRACY

24 LUDWIG VON MISES

1881–1973

As one of the leaders of the Austrian School of Economics, Ludwig von Mises was one of the greatest free-market libertarian economists of the 20th century.

Born to a Jewish family in Austria-Hungary, at the age of 12 Ludwig spoke fluent Yiddish, German, Polish and French, read Latin, and could speak conversational Ukrainian. Fearing the German invasion of Switzerland, in 1940 von Mises emigrated to New York, upon which he became a visiting professor at New York University, a position he held until his retirement.

Von Mises' greatest contribution was his argument that socialism must fail due to the 'economic calculation problem'; arguing that it is impossible for a socialist government to organize a complex economy due to a lack of a functional price system. He believed that a functional price system was an essential signalling mechanism in order to rationally allocate goods.

Von Mises believed that in a capitalist society, prices are set by private owners of production, who maintain their capital when they allocate it efficiently, and liquidate or become bankrupt when they fail to allocate their capital efficiently. In a socialist society, however, capital is allocated not according to the most efficient distribution, but instead based upon interpersonal comparisons of utility according to the views of the theoretical socialist planner. Hence with Socialism lacking these price mechanism-fuelled passages of capital, von Mises argued that socialism must fail: demand cannot be known without prices.

Furthering this, von Mises believed in the 'sovereignty of the consumer' and that it is the consumer that ultimately dictates the way a society should develop; "...the consumers determine precisely what should be produced, in what quality, and in what quantities...they are merciless egoistic bosses, full of whims and fancies, changeable and unpredictable".

"THE ONLY CERTAIN FACT ABOUT RUSSIAN AFFAIRS UNDER THE SOVIET REGIME WITH REGARD TO WHICH ALL PEOPLE AGREE IS: THAT THE STANDARD OF LIVING OF THE RUSSIAN MASSES IS MUCH LOWER THAN THAT OF THE MASSES IN THE COUNTRY WHICH IS UNIVERSALLY CONSIDERED AS THE PARAGON OF CAPITALISM, THE UNITED STATES OF AMERICA. IF WE WERE TO REGARD THE SOVIET REGIME AS AN EXPERIMENT, WE WOULD HAVE TO SAY THAT THE EXPERIMENT HAS CLEARLY DEMONSTRATED THE SUPERIORITY OF CAPITALISM AND THE INFERIORITY OF SOCIALISM."

LUDWIG VON MISES FROM SOCIALISM

25 JOHN MAYNARD KEYNES
1883–1946

Perhaps not many people came out of the 2008 financial crisis in as good condition as the legacy of John Maynard Keynes.

Born in 1883 to a middle class family in Cambridge, Keynes was schooled at Eton before attending the University of Cambridge. After a brief career in the civil service, Keynes returned to Cambridge, which he would consider his base for the rest of his life. A decorated war hero for his economic work at the Treasury helping to finance World War 1, Keynes' first major public appearance was during the Treaty of Versailles, where he argued that the high compensation package being exerted upon Germany, if set too high, would not only make a German economic recovery unattainable, but would also damage the wider economy.

Whilst unsuccessful at the time, the collapse of the Weimar Republic and the rise of Hitler's National Socialist German Workers party (aka 'Nazi' party) ultimately proved Keynes correct. The Treaty of Versailles may have raised Keynes' public profile, but it was during the Great Depression that he achieved widespread fame. Keynes had begun theorizing the relationship between unemployment, money and prices, detailing counter cyclical public spending and synthesizing ideas surrounding the multiplier effect (where an initial change can have a greater final impact on equilibrium national income). In essence, Keynes advocated for a 'mixed economy', believing that during a recession a government should spend its way out by stimulating economic growth, and during a boom, governments should spend wisely and save for the inevitable bust.

In 1944 Keynes led the British delegation to the Bretton Woods conference, during which he played a pivotal role in the formulation of the International Monetary Fund (IMF) and the World Bank.

On both sides of the Atlantic, Keynes' was taken very seriously, with the 'Keynesian revolution' following the publication of his hugely influential *General Theory of Employment, Interest and Money*. Widely considered to be the father of modern macroeconomics, Keynes' model acted as the chief economic model towards the end of the Great Depression, World War 2 and the 'Age of Keynes' (1945–1973).

Most Keynesians advocate an activist stabilization policy to reduce the amplitude of the business cycle, which they rank among the most serious of economic problems.

Since the 2008 global financial crisis there has been a 'Keynesian resurgence' amongst economists and policy makers as Keynes' response to the Great Depression (notably fiscal stimulus and robust government intervention) has moved firmly back into the spotlight.

"OWE YOUR BANKER £1,000 AND YOU ARE AT HIS MERCY; OWE HIM £1M AND THE POSITION IS REVERSED."
KEYNES ON DEBT, INDEPENDENT.CO.UK

"MARKETS CAN REMAIN IRRATIONAL A LOT LONGER THAT YOU AND I CAN REMAIN SOLVENT."
KEYNES ON INVESTING FROM FORBES

"IF ECONOMISTS COULD MANAGE TO GET THEMSELVES THOUGHT OF AS HUMBLE, COMPETENT PEOPLE ON A LEVEL WITH DENTISTS, THAT WOULD BE SPLENDID."

KEYNES FROM ESSAYS IN PERSUASION

26 HARRY DEXTER WHITE

1892–1948

The case of Harry Dexter White provides undoubtedly one of the most controversial stories in economics, finance and global foreign policy.

As one of the leading American economists and Statesmen during World War 2, White's deep involvement at the 1944 Bretton Woods meeting enabled him, alongside British economist John Maynard Keynes, to formulate the design and implementation of the International Monetary Fund (IMF) and the World Bank.

Armed with a PhD in economics from Harvard, White rose to become chief economist at the US Treasury. During World War 2, White played a key role in the development of the 'Morgenthau Plan'; a plan involving the dismantling of German industry and the internationalization of its activities. Clearly, White's positions throughout his career gave him access to an extensive range of confidential information about the US and its allies.

In spite of this, not only was White the US Treasury's top economist, but he was also one of the Soviet Union's most valuable spies…

…Starting from the 1940s onwards, a series of soviet defectors increasingly began naming a 'Mr White' as a source of confidential information to the Soviets. White's double life as both the US Treasury's top economist whilst facilitating espionage activities for the Soviet Union was catching up with him.

In late 1948, White testified before a US court, denying being a communist. White died only a few days later from a heart attack.

Two years after his death, in 1950 the FBI positively identified White as a Soviet spy, operating under the codenames 'Jurist'. And with that the US's top economist, instrumental throughout World War 2 and pivotal in the formation of the IMF and World Bank, was exposed.

"IT WOULD SEEM TO BE AN IMPORTANT STEP IN THE DIRECTION OF WORLD STABILITY IF A MEMBER GOVERNMENT COULD OBTAIN THE FULL COOPERATION OF OTHER MEMBER GOVERNMENTS IN THE CONTROL OF CAPITAL FLOWS. "

WHITE'S ATTEMPTS TO PROMOTE INCREASED IMF TRADE WITH THE SOVIET UNION, DESPITE THE SOVIET ECONOMIC SYSTEM BEING OPPOSED TO OPEN TRADE AND FINANCE, 1942.

"THE MOST HIGHLY-PLACED ASSET THE SOVIETS POSSESSED IN THE AMERICAN GOVERNMENT."

HAYNES, KLEHR AND VASSILIEV, 2009

27 SIDNEY WEINBERG

1891–1969

In 1907, a 16 year old high school dropout from Brooklyn walked into a brokerage house in New York asking for a job as a janitor's assistant, paying $3 per hour. Twenty-three years later that same man became CEO of the brokerage firm. The firm's name? Goldman Sachs.

The story of Sidney Weinberg stands as perhaps the most inspirational 'rags-to-riches' story in the history of finance. The son of a Jewish wholesale liquor dealer, Weinberg left school aged 15 before landing his first proper job as a janitor at Goldman Sachs. His main duties were to polish the partners' shoes and to brush their hats and coats. The grandson of the firm's founder, Paul Sachs took a shine to Weinberg, promoting him to the mailroom, which Weinberg subsequently transformed through the implementation of much more efficient practises.

The firm sent Weinberg to the Brooklyn Business College to improve his penmanship, and following his duties in the US Navy during World War 1, Weinberg was made a securities trader for the firm in 1925. Rising rapidly through the ranks, by 1927 he was made a partner, and by 1930 he was CEO.

Hugely charismatic, Weinberg was dubbed 'Mr Wall Street' for his enviable address book, charm and persona; almost every American CEO was good friends with Weinberg. In an industry traditionally dominated by smart, ivy-league educated bankers, Weinberg was proud to be the only 'ex-Brooklyn newspaper seller' on Wall Street, making jokes and references to his humble background as often as he could.

Weinberg remained CEO of the firm for a remarkable 39 years, transforming it from a mid-tier brokerage house into the world's most prestigious investment bank. No other individual comes close to being as influential in the success of Goldman Sachs as Weinberg.

> **PROUDLY PRONOUNCING HIS NAME 'WINE-BOIG', THROUGHOUT HIS LIFE HE HAD SCARS ON HIS BACK FROM KNIFE FIGHTS IN HIS YOUTH.**

"OUR NATION IS IN GRAVE DANGER. AMERICA NEEDS AN ENORMOUS NUMBER OF TALENTED EXECUTIVE LEADERS TO ORGANIZE A MASSIVE WAR PRODUCTION EFFORT. THE PRESIDENT HAS SENT ME HERE TO GET YOUR HELP IN IDENTIFYING YOUR VERY BEST YOUNG MEN. WE NEED THE SMARTEST YOUNG STARS YOU'VE GOT. AND DON'T EVEN THINK OF PASSING OFF OLDER MEN OR SECOND-RATERS. I'M ASKING THE SAME THING OF EVERY MAJOR COMPANY IN THE COUNTRY, AND I'LL BE WATCHING VERY CLOSELY HOW WELL YOUR MEN DO COMPARED TO THE BEST YOUNG MEN FROM ALL THE OTHER CORPORATIONS. GOD FORBID THE PEOPLE YOU PICK ARE LESS THAN THE BEST BECAUSE GOD, PRESIDENT ROOSEVELT, AND I WOULD NEVER, EVER FORGIVE YOU."

WEINBERG WHILST RECRUITING FOR THE WAR PRODUCTION BOARD DURING WORLD WAR 2 IN 1941

AT HIS PRIME HE SERVED ON 31 CORPORATE BOARDS AND ATTENDED 251 BOARD MEETINGS PER YEAR.

28 GEORGES DORIOT

1899–1987

An ever increasing number of today's modern corporate successes share a common denominator; venture capital.

Facebook? Apple Inc? Twitter? LinkedIn? Well it all started with a French, ex-US military, Harvard professor called Georges Doriot…

…Doriot returned to Harvard University following the end of World War 2, upon which he founded the American Research and Development Corporation (ARDC); the first publicly owned venture capital firm. As a decorated war veteran himself, the firm's main aim was to encourage private sector investments in start-up businesses run by World War 2 veterans. Crucially, ARDC was the first private equity investment firm that accepted money from sources other than wealthy individuals.

Bridging the gap between cash-poor entrepreneurs and the institutional investment community, ARDC's philosophy was to take calculated risks in selected growth companies. Essentially, Doriot viewed the investor–entrepreneur bond to be that of a father–child relationship; with the role of the investor being to nurture the entrepreneur's dreams as oppose to simply providing the finance with which to let them try to build a company. Doriot often said that "a history of profits is much more important in the long run than a profit in any one year".

Doriot's ARDC was responsible for the first major venture capital success story when its 1957 investment of $70,000 in Digital Equipment Corporation (DEC) grew to become valued at over $355 million at the company's IPO 11 years later.

Doriot paved the way for the venture capital industry, which has since developed to become crucial for providing vital fuel to give fledgling companies the drive that they need to survive their adolescence.

> # "WITHOUT ACTIONS THE WORLD WOULD STILL BE AN IDEA."
>
> *GEORGES DORIOT FROM THE FIRST VENTURE CAPITALIST*

> # "A CREATIVE MAN MERELY HAS IDEAS; A RESOURCEFUL MAN MAKES THEM PRACTICAL."
>
> *GEORGES DORIOT FROM CREATIVE CAPITAL*

"ALWAYS REMEMBER THAT SOMEONE, SOMEWHERE, IS MAKING A PRODUCT THAT WILL MAKE YOUR PRODUCT OBSOLETE."

GEORGES DORIOT FROM CREATIVE CAPITAL

29 BENJAMIN GRAHAM

1894–1976

On 16th December 1954, Warren Buffett's first son was born; Howard Graham Buffett. 'Howard' was in homage to Buffett's father, but to whom was 'Graham' attributable? Who could be so influential to Warren Buffett that he would choose to include him in the naming of his first-born son?

Benjamin Graham, the acclaimed economist and investor, is widely known as the father of 'value investing'. Following his graduation from Columbia University, Graham headed to Wall Street, where he began one of the most profound investing careers for generations to come. It was Graham who taught Buffett how to stock pick, and became his teacher and mentor throughout his life.

In short, Graham's 'value investing' strategy teaches investors to value a stock principally as a representation of a part-ownership of a business, where the owner should not be overly concerned with short-term movements in share price.

Graham's approach proposed that whilst, in the short term, the stock market essentially behaves like a voting machine, in the long run it behaves more like a weighing machine (where the stock's true value will be reflected in its price). Famously, Graham used the analogy of 'Mr Market' in order to portray his value investing strategy:

Imagine that every day, Mr Market arrives at the investor's door offering to buy or sell shares at a specific price. Mr Market's price often varies; sometimes he is reasonable, whilst sometimes his prices are irrational. Each day, no obligation is placed on the investor to do any business with Mr Market.

Because of Mr Market's daily irrationalities the investor should not determine the value of their shares by simply considering the price offered that day by Mr Market, instead the investor should largely ignore the day-to-day behaviour of Mr Market, whilst concentrating on the real life performance of that company, in addition to receiving dividends. Patience, Graham therefore argued, was critical.

Now widely believed amongst the investing community, Graham proposed that a 'margin of safety' exists when a company's stock trades at a price that is discounted to its intrinsic value, at which point investment should occur.

"I READ THE FIRST EDITION OF HIS
BOOK EARLY IN 1950, WHEN I WAS 19.
I THOUGHT THEN THAT IT WAS BY FAR
THE BEST BOOK ABOUT INVESTING EVER
WRITTEN. I STILL THINK IT IS."

WARREN BUFFETT FROM THE INTELLIGENT INVESTOR

"INDIVIDUALS WHO CANNOT MASTER THEIR EMOTIONS ARE ILL-SUITED TO PROFIT FROM THE INVESTMENT PROCESS."

GRAHAM FROM LESSONS FROM EXPERT TRADERS

"TO ACHIEVE SATISFACTORY INVESTMENT RESULTS IS EASIER THAN MOST PEOPLE REALIZE BUT TO ACHIEVE SUPERIOR RESULTS IS HARDER THAN IT LOOKS."

GRAHAM FROM THE INTELLIGENT INVESTOR

"OBVIOUS PROSPECTS FOR PHYSICAL GROWTH IN A BUSINESS DO NOT TRANSLATE INTO OBVIOUS PROFITS FOR INVESTORS."

GRAHAM FROM THE INTELLIGENT INVESTOR

30 ALFRED WINSLOW JONES

1900–1989

Think you know all about hedge funds, right? Well let's have a look at how it all started…

The journalist-turned-fund manager, Dr Alfred W. Jones, is widely credited as the godfather of the hedge fund industry and the creator of the world's first hedge fund.

A journalist for *Fortune* magazine, Jones identified that price fluctuations of individual stocks consisted of two components; that which is attributable to the individual asset's performance, and that of the market. By treating these as two separate concepts Jones structured an investment vehicle that attempted to minimize the risks associated with holding long-term stock positions; by purchasing assets whose price he expected to rise, and 'short selling' those that he expected to fall. In doing this, Jones' fund was able to subdue the overall market effects on the individual asset; if stocks went down, the losses on his long stocks would be offset by gains on his short assets, and vice versa. He charged no fee unless a profit was made.

REVOLUTIONARY AT THE TIME, BY FUSING LEVERAGE (TO BUY MORE SHARES) WITH SHORT SELLING (TO MINIMIZE MARKET-WIDE DOWNTURNS), THE PERFORMANCE OF THE FUND WOULD NO LONGER BE RELIANT UPON THE DIRECTION OF THE MARKET *PER SE*, BUT ON THE QUALITY OF THE STOCKS PICKED BY THE MANAGER.

With this, the 'hedge fund' was born – protecting risk on both sides through 'hedging'.

Achieving growth of 17.3% in its first year, Jones' invention led to positive returns in 31 out of its 34 year life. From Jones' $100,000 initial investment, the hedge fund industry has matured into a $3 trillion plus industry.

Today of course, hedge funds vary widely, with each having their own investment strategy that determines which type of investments they participate in. Hedge fund strategies have evolved to include a variety of activities such as global macro, directional and event-driven to invest in, amongst others, equity, fixed income, commodities money market instruments and debt.

INVESTMENT MANAGEMENT WAS JONES' FIFTH CAREER WHEN HE STARTED A.W. JONES & CO AT THE AGE OF 48.

LATER IN HIS LIFE, JONES TRIED TO ESTABLISH A 'REVERSE PEACE CORPS', WHEREBY US AID RECIPIENTS WOULD SEND THEIR OWN VOLUNTEERS TO WORK WITH THE POOR COMMUNITY OF THE USA, AS A WAY OF 'HEDGING' AGAINST A CULTURE OF INFERIORITY AMONGST DEVELOPING COUNTRIES.

31 DENG XIAOPING

1904–1997

Deng Xiaoping, the Chinese statesman, was undoubtedly one of China's chief architects of economic reforms and socialist modernization. Deng opened China to foreign investment, the global economy and private competition. Deng's influence allowed China to become one of the world's fastest growing and most powerful economies, dramatically raising the quality of life of a vast amount of the Chinese population.

Born into a peasant family in 1904, Deng studied and worked in 1920s France, where he became influenced by Marxism. Upon his return to China, Deng joined the Communist Party of China in 1923.

Whilst Deng officially became a part of the Marxist revolutionary movement in China, he was actually much more of a nationalist. Desperate to see China stand equally with the great global players, Deng felt that participation in the communist movement was the only feasible route to Chinese nationalism.

He rose through the ranks of China's governing elite, and in the years following Chairman Mao's death in 1976, Deng emerged as the de-facto leader of China.

"...A PRIMARY ARCHITECT OF CHINA'S MODERNIZATION AND DRAMATIC ECONOMIC DEVELOPMENT."

THEN-UN SECRETARY-GENERAL KOFI ANNAN DESCRIBING DENG IN 1997

Under Deng's rule, he facilitated increasing free speech domestically, and elevated China onto the global political stage. He initiated wide-ranging social, political and economic reforms by turning away from many traditional communist principles and applying free market ideals into the Chinese system. Negotiating the return of Hong Kong from the British, and the return of Macau from the Portuguese, Deng embarked upon a global tour with a key aim of communicating to the world that China's key priorities were economic reform and technological development.

Deng's trademark (albeit contested), motto *'to get rich is glorious'* released a groundswell of entrepreneurship and innovation within a nation historically associated with central planning and communism.

Deng's economic liberalization led to the phenomenal economic growth in the coastal areas of China, and to the development of Shanghai's Pudong New Area, revitalizing the city as both a national and a global economic hub.

Deng died in 1997 aged 92.

"DO NOT CARE IF THE CAT IS BLACK OR WHITE. WHAT MATTERS IS IT CATCHES MICE."

DENG XIAOPING SPEAKING ON CAPITALISM VS COMMUNISM, 1961

32 PETER DRUCKER

1909–2005

Should we view employees as 'assets' or 'liabilities'? 'Key sources of competitive advantage' or simply 'resources' that a business uses to make money with?

Widely regarded as the 'man who invented management' (and later the 'godfather of management consulting') Peter Drucker was one of the first people to explore the methods by which humans organize themselves within a corporation. Drucker pioneered many of the concepts that were to later develop in the 20th century; predicting privatization, decentralization, the rise of Japan as an economic superpower, innovation and the importance of lifelong learning by the 'knowledge worker' within an information society. Drucker wrote 39 books and a multitude of academic articles and reports.

Influenced by Joseph Schumpeter (a close friend of his father), Drucker saw innovation and entrepreneurship within the organization as crucial to its long-term success. Growing up in mainland Europe during a period of great

IN THE EARLY 1970S, DRUCKER DEVELOPED ONE OF THE WORLD'S FIRST MBA PROGRAMMES AT CLAREMONT.

political unrest and conflict, Drucker found hope in what he considered to be the near-endless possibilities that the modern corporation could provide in value-creating and community development.

Believing that "an organization is a human, a social, indeed a moral phenomenon", Drucker emphasized that it is the manager's job to prepare and to organize the workforce; emphasizing decentralization and simplification over command and control. In essence, Drucker argued that the role of the manager is not to dictate to their employees, but to create the right working environment within which employees, an organization's most valuable resource, can flourish.

Drucker's breakthrough 1946 book *Concept of the Corporation* was based on his first-hand observations gained during his two year 'political audit' of General Motors (GM), one of the world's largest companies at the time. Before Drucker, such a report would have concentrated solely on mechanical processes such as accounting, cash flow and engineering, however, Drucker chose to go beyond such practises; attending board meetings, interviewing employees and analysing GMs top managers, and evaluating the firm's internal working relations and disciplines. The result was a groundbreaking development in the way in which society, corporate valuers and potential acquirors now view a corporation.

Seeing large organizations as more than simply numbers and mechanical processes, Drucker believed that the 'corporation' should be hailed as one of mankind's greatest inventions.

> ## "I SUDDENLY REALIZED THAT KEYNES AND ALL THE BRILLIANT ECONOMIC STUDENTS IN THE ROOM WERE INTERESTED IN THE BEHAVIOUR OF COMMODITIES, WHILE I WAS INTERESTED IN THE BEHAVIOUR OF PEOPLE."
>
> *DRUCKER DESCRIBING A 1934 LECTURE GIVEN IN CAMBRIDGE BY JOHN MAYNARD KEYNES*

"WHENEVER YOU SEE A SUCCESSFUL BUSINESS, SOMEONE ONCE MADE A COURAGEOUS DECISION."

DRUCKER FROM THE LITTLE BOOK OF BIG DECISIONS

"THE THREE MOST CHARISMATIC LEADERS IN THIS CENTURY INFLICTED MORE SUFFERING ON THE HUMAN RACE THAT ALMOST ANY TRIO IN HISTORY: HITLER, STALIN AND MAO. WHAT MATTERS IS NOT THE LEADER'S CHARISMA. WHAT MATTERS IS THE LEADER'S MISSION."

DRUCKER FROM MANAGING THE NON-PROFIT ORGANIZATION

33 RONALD REAGAN

1911–2004

Q
What do you get when you take a former TV and film actor, make him the President of the United States and allow him to apply his own personal economic ethos to the largest economy in the world?

A
The greatest sustained wave of economic prosperity that the US had ever seen.

Former Hollywood actor Ronald Reagan, the 40th President of the United States, presided over the longest peacetime economic expansion the US had ever experienced.

With an emphasis on federal monetary policy, privatization, deregulation, 'trickle-down' economics and an expansion of free trade, Reagan facilitated major reforms to the US economy. So influential were his economic policies that they have become known as 'Reaganomics'.

Essentially, Reaganomics was supply-side, laissez-faire economics, consisting of four pillars; reducing the growth of government spending, reducing income tax and capital gains tax, reducing government regulation and controlling the money supply to reduce inflation.

Reagan believed that it was the private sector, not the government, that provided the fuel with which the US economy would be driven. In 1981, when the US air traffic controllers union (PATCO) went on strike Regan simply announced that those who did not return to their jobs within 48 hours would be fired. Forty-eight hours later, 11,345 air traffic controllers had lost their jobs. Reagan wanted to show America that he did not fear unions.

Under the Reagan administration, the US economy went from a GDP growth of approximately −0.3% (in 1980) to 4.1% (in 1988).

Often reported to have taken very little notes in meetings (before being able to recite intricate details to near perfection days later), Reagan's ability to grasp complex economic concepts and then 'translate' them into laymans terms are said to be one of his greatest attributes.

"FREEDOM IS NEVER MORE THAN ONE GENERATION AWAY FROM EXTINCTION. WE DIDN'T PASS IT TO OUR CHILDREN IN THE BLOODSTREAM. IT MUST BE FOUGHT FOR, PROTECTED, AND HANDED ON FOR THEM TO DO THE SAME."

REAGAN FROM HIS ADDRESS TO THE ANNUAL MEETING OF THE PHOENIX CHAMBER OF COMMERCE IN MARCH 1961

"ENTREPRENEURS AND THEIR SMALL ENTERPRISES ARE RESPONSIBLE FOR ALMOST ALL THE ECONOMIC GROWTH IN THE UNITED STATES."

REAGAN FROM HIS MAY 1988 SPEECH TO STUDENTS AT MOSCOW UNIVERSITY WHO WERE MEMBERS OF THE YOUNG COMMUNIST LEAGUE

"ONE PICTURE IS WORTH 1,000 DENIALS."

*REAGAN TO THE WHITE HOUSE NEWS
PHOTOGRAPHERS ASSOCIATION, MAY 18, 1983*

"INFLATION IS AS VIOLENT AS A MUGGER,
AS FRIGHTENING AS AN ARMED ROBBER
AND AS DEADLY AS A HITMAN."

REAGAN AT A FUNDRAISING DINNER IN 1978

34 BERNARD CORNFELD

1927–1995

Bernard 'Bernie' Cornfeld represents one of history's most flamboyant figures in international finance.

Moving from Turkey to America aged four, following World War 2, Cornfeld began working as a social worker, before joining a mutual fund company.

With only a few hundred dollars in savings, in 1955 Cornfeld moved to Paris and set up his own mutual fund company, called Investors Overseas Services (IOS). The company targeted American servicemen in Europe, allowing Cornfeld to avoid both European and American tax regulation. Intially, IOS mostly sold shares in the 'Dreyfus Fund' (a fund managed by a close friend).

Cornfeld's IOS was incredibly successful; at its peak it employed over 25,000 people and raised over $2.5 billion in just under ten years.

Calling it 'people's capitalism', Cornfeld's IOS provided US expatriates with low-levels of capital with access to mainstream US investing (which previously required relatively high capital commitments).

Cornfeld became famous both in the financial world and beyond – wild parties, lavish houses and a string of celebrity girlfriends fuelled the media's interest in him.

> ## "DO YOU SINCERELY WANT TO BE RICH?"
>
> *CORNFELD'S FAMOUS ONE-LINE PITCH*

In many ways, Cornfeld became a victim of his own success. So confident was Cornfeld that his personal mantra became centred on the belief that mutual funds should take their fees from the profits they make, not just a percentage of the assets they manage. Clever marketing at the time… in a bull market that is…

In the bear market of 1969, Cornfeld's IOS fund took a serious hit, and by April 1969 IOS was quickly running out of money. At this point, American financier Robert Vesco stepped in, resulting in the eventual eviction of Cornfeld from IOS, the collapse of the company and the undoing of a number of banks also.

Questionably with the support of Vesco, Cornfeld spent 11 months in prison for fraud allegations committed whilst at IOS.

"I HAD MANSIONS ALL OVER THE WORLD, I THREW EXTRAVAGANT PARTIES AND I LIVED WITH TEN OR TWELVE GIRLS AT A TIME."

CORNFELD FROM TREASURE ISLANDS

"EVER SINCE THE SOUTH SEA BUBBLE, WHICH FINALLY BURST IN 1720, THERE HAS NEVER BEEN A LACK OF INVESTORS WILLING TO PUT THEIR MONEY INTO A COLOURFULLY PRESENTED SCHEME TO MAKE MONEY QUICKLY...BUT NOTHING COULD HAVE BEEN MORE SPECTACULAR THAN THE RISE AND FALL OF BERNIE CORNFELD."

CORNFELD'S OBITUARY: THE INDEPENDENT, MARCH 1995

35 ROBERT VESCO

1935–2007

For four years in a row, Robert Lee Vesco was listed on *Forbes'* wealthiest people in the world report. His occupation? According to *Forbes'*; Thief.

Born the son of a Detroit autoworker in 1935, Vesco grew up to live one of finance's most colourful careers. Vesco maintained that he always had three goals in life: "To get the Hell out of Detroit, be president of a corporation and become a millionaire!" Soon after dropping out of engineering school in his early 20s he had achieved all three.

Initially joining an investment firm, Vesco entered into the aluminium broking industry. Through a series of highly leveraged hostile takeovers and debt-fuelled expansions, his business, International Controls Corporation, grew rapidly. By age 33, Vesco's stake in ICC was worth over $50 million.

In 1970, Vesco mounted a successful takeover bid for a $1.5 billion Swiss-based offshore mutual fund called Investor Overseas Services. A cocktail of high leverage, creative accounting and corporate greed turned the deal nasty when the founder (Bernard Cornfeld) was jailed and Vesco was accused of stealing hundreds of millions of dollars from the company. To make matters worse, not only was the scandal one of the largest frauds in history, but it involved many high profile figures in finance, business, politics and even royalty.

Vesco fled, taking with him $200 million (close to $1 billion in today's terms). For the next 35 years, Vesco drifted between many Caribbean islands, earning his nickname of 'the undisputed king of the fugitive financiers'.

During his life on-the-run, Vesco was to become involved in drug trafficking, money laundering, making an illegal contribution to Richard Nixon's 1972 presidential reelection campaign, attempting

IN THE LATE 1970S, VESCO UNSUCCESSFULLY TRIED TO BUY AN OUTLYING ISLAND OFF THE COAST OF ANTIGUA. HE REPORTEDLY BELIEVED THAT FROM THERE, HE COULD ESTABLISH HIS OWN COUNTRY, THUS AVOIDING AN EXTRADITION TO THE US.

to set up his own country in the Caribbean and plotting to bribe US officials to allow Libya to buy American military planes. In Costa Rica, Vesco donated large sums of money to the President, resulting in an extradition embargo, later to become known as the 'Vesco Law'.

In 1982, Vesco settled in Cuba, where he grew a beard and lived under the alias of a Canadian citizen named 'Tom Adams'. His precise activities in Cuba are unclear, however, he is reported to have been involved in helping Fidel Castro and the Cuban government to set up trading companies to circumvent the US embargo. In the 1990s, Vesco, Donald Nixon (Richard Nixon's nephew) and Fidel and Raul Castro began conducting clinical trials on a 'wonderdrug' which claimed to boost immunity. However, on 31st May 1995, Vesco reportedly attempted to defraud Nixon and Castro, resulting in his arrest.

Sentenced to 13 years in a Cuban jail for 'fraud and illicit economic activity', Vesco died of lung cancer in 2007.

VESCO OWNED A PRIVATE BOEING 707 JET, THE 'SILVER PHYLLIS', COMPLETE WITH AN ON-BOARD SAUNA AND A DISCO. THE ONLY OTHER PRIVATE BOEING 707 AT THE TIME BELONGED TO THE US PRESIDENT, 'AIR FORCE ONE'.

36 HYMAN MINSKY

1919–1996

Is our economy just a big Ponzi scheme? Just how stable really is 'stability'?

The US economist Hyman Minsky is most famous for his theories on financial market fragility and debt accumulation, arguing that what we might consider 'stable' is in fact inherently destabilizing.

Minksy's work centred on the belief that during prosperous times (i.e. unusually long periods of economic 'stability'), a speculative level of excitement develops, where investors are lured into taking on more and more debt. Eventually, this accumulation of debt will lead to excessive levels of borrowing, which will in turn produce a financial crisis.

Minsky identified three main types of borrower, increasingly risky in nature. The *'hedge borrower'* can meet all debt payments (interest and principle) from their cash flows. The *'speculative borrower'* is a step further out on the risk profile by being able to service their debt (i.e. meet the interest payments), but having to regularly 'roll' the debt to repay the original loan. The *'Ponzi borrower'* (named after Charles Ponzi) can repay neither the interest or the original debt, and instead they rely upon the appreciation of the asset's value to repay the debt.

Minsky argued that the longer the period of economic 'stability' lasts, the more the economy moves towards being full of Ponzi borrowers until eventually the economy becomes a house of cards, built upon excessive speculation and easy credit. When the bubble eventually bursts and asset prices stop rising, a domino effect is created; whereby the Ponzi borrowers cause the collapse of the speculative borrowers, which then cause the collapse of the hedge borrowers (despite the reliability of their underlying investments).

MINKSY RECEIVED HIS PHD IN ECONOMICS FROM HARVARD, WHERE HE STUDIED UNDER JOSEPH SCHUMPETER.

A 'MINSKY MOMENT' OCCURS WHEN OVER-INDEBTED INVESTORS ARE FORCED TO SELL GOOD ASSETS TO PAY BACK THEIR LOANS, CAUSING SHARP DECLINES IN FINANCIAL MARKETS AND JUMPS IN DEMAND FOR CASH.

"IT IS TO RECOGNIZE THAT THE FINANCIAL SYSTEM IS BOTH NECESSARY AND DANGEROUS, THAT STRICT FINANCIAL REGULATION IS BOTH INDISPENSIBLE AND IMPERFECT."

JAMES GALBRAITH'S KEYNOTE LECTURE TO THE 5TH ANNUAL DIJON CONFERENCE ON POST KEYNESIAN ECONOMICS AT ROSKILDE UNIVERSTITY NEAR COPENHAGEN IN MAY 2011

37 HENRY KRAVIS

B.1944

It's hard to say the phrase 'private equity' without thinking of Henry Kravis. Kravis was a pioneer in the development of the 'Leveraged Buyout' (LBO) and the private equity boom that spread across America during the late 1970s and 1980s.

Born in 1944 in Oklahoma, Kravis received his MBA from Columbia Business School before embarking upon a career that was to dominate both the financial press and the society magazines for years. Initially working for Bear Stearns, Kravis was made partner at the impressively young age of 30. It was there where he first began experimenting with 'bootstrap' investments, including the first significant LBO.

Despite his success, rising tensions at Bear Stearns resulted in Kravis, along with his cousin George Roberts and mentor Jerome Kohlberg Jr, leaving in 1976 to form Kohlberg Kravis Roberts (KKR).

Assisted by Michael Milken and the high-yield bond phenomena, KKR rapidly became a dominant player. The very public battle for control at RJR Nabisco in 1989, eventually won by KKR for a price of $25 billion, placed the LBO industry firmly in the spotlight. Today, KKR boasts many of the landmark achievements in private equity, including the first buyout of a public company by tender offer, the first billion dollar buyout, the largest buyout in US history and the largest buyout in European history.

Kravis is reported to have led a colourful career both in and out of the office, with his wealth estimated at $5.1 billion. He earned $370 million in 2007 alone. Today, Kravis has houses in New York, The Hamptons, Palm Beach, Paris, Colorado and Connecticut. Away from the office, Kravis is an active philanthropist, having donated hundreds of millions of dollars to charitable causes over his lifetime.

"SO I PICKED A FIELD WHERE I HAD A LITTLE EXPOSURE. WHERE I THOUGHT I COULD HAVE AN ENORMOUS CHALLENGE, AND HAVE A CHANCE TO REALLY DO SOME GOOD, TO BE A PIONEER IN AN AREA, AND NOT JUST BE LIKE EVERYONE ELSE."

KRAVIS ON HIS INVOLVEMENT IN THE CREATION OF THE PRIVATE EQUITY INDUSTRY IN AN INTERVIEW WITH THE ACADEMY OF ACHIEVEMENT IN 1991

"DON'T CONGRATULATE ME WHEN I BUY A COMPANY, CONGRATULATE ME WHEN I SELL IT. ANY FOOL CAN OVERPAY AND BUY A COMPANY."

HENRY KRAVIS FROM PRIVATE EQUITY EXITS

38 MICHAEL MILKEN

B.1946

The 'Junk Bond King' Michael Milken was an American bond trader, famed for his role in the development of the market for high-yield bonds during the 1970s and 1980s. Whilst many have described him as the embodiment of 1980s Wall Street greed, many have credited Milken with fuelling much of America's economic growth through his use of bonds and hybrids, leading to what is today a major part of the structure of global finance.

Whilst studying at university, Milken observed that conventional bond rating systems largely relied upon a firm's past performance and its debt-to-equity ratio, identifying that through risk-adjustment and a revision of the bond rating system (to include cash flow, human resources, corporate objectives and strategy), low-grade bonds could indeed provide a worthwhile risk.

Upon leaving university Milken joined at Drexel Burnham Lambert, initially starting as a low-grade bond researcher. Milken was so dedicated to his work that in his first year he reportedly wore a miner's headlamp whilst commuting on the bus to enable him to read company accounts before work. Milken implemented the now-famous 'X' shaped trading floors; believing that this enabled maximum dynamics between traders and salesmen.

Milken's reputation in the market enabled him to build up an enviable network of bond buyers – if money needed to be raised quickly, Milken was the man to do it. Milken's (now infamous) 'highly confident letter' (in which Milken pledged to raise the necessary debt required) facilitated the wave of Leveraged Buyouts (LBOs) to occur throughout 1980s corporate America. Legend has it that on one occasion Milken raised $1 billion for MCI Communications in less than an hour. Entrepreneurs such as

> "ANY ANALYSIS OF CAPITAL STRUCTURE SHOULD RECOGNIZE THAT MOST BALANCE SHEETS ARE DRAMATICALLY INACCURATE BECAUSE (WITH THE EXCEPTION OF PROFESSIONAL SPORTS FRANCHISES) THEY FAIL TO INCLUDE THE VALUE OF HUMAN CAPITAL."
>
> *MILKEN FROM MIKEMILKEN.COM*

Steve Wynn, John Malone and Ted Turner owe at least part of their early success to Milken's fundraising capabilities.

At the height of his success, Milken was reported to be earning over $500 million per year. In 17 years of trading bonds, Milken reportedly had only four losing months.

However, the music stopped on 24th April 1990, when Milken pleaded guilty to charges brought against him regarding securities, reporting and tax violations. Milken served 22 months in prison.

Upon his release from prison (and successfully overcoming prostate cancer) Milken has dedicated a large part of his life to fundraising for medical research, with *Fortune* magazine calling him 'The Man Who Changed Medicine' in 2004.

"IN THE 1920S, WHEN AUTOMOBILES BECAME A HUGE INDUSTRY, 60% OF THE COST OF PRODUCING A CAR WAS IN RAW MATERIALS AND ENERGY. FOR TODAY'S COMPUTER CHIPS IT'S LESS THAN 2% OF THE COST. BRAINPOWER HAS BECOME THE 'RAW MATERIAL' FOR BUILDING COMPANIES. THIS HUMAN CAPITAL, COMBINED WITH THE SOCIAL CAPITAL OF DEMOCRACY, OPEN MARKETS AND THE RULE OF LAW – IS THE BASIS OF A PROSPEROUS ECONOMY."

MILKEN FROM MIKEMILKEN.COM

39 MURRAY ROTHBARD

1926–1995

Most of us agree that a government, in some form, should exist in any modern, civilized society. Let's face it, without a government, there would just be anarchy, right? Not necessarily…

If you think about it, a government is essentially just another monopoly provider of goods and services. The ultimate monopoly provider if you wish. And aren't we taught that the lack of competition faced by monopolies just makes them complacent and inefficient?

These were the well-documented views of Murray Rothbard, the self proclaimed 'Anarcho-Capitalist'. Raised in a right wing family within a relatively communist neighbourhood in New York's Bronx district, Rothbard rose to become a prominent member of the Austrian School of Economics. Throughout his life, Rothbard was a defiant defender of the freedom of the individual against government intervention. He believed that the freemarket produced widespread wealth, social cohesion and economic prosperity for everyone within society, and that government intervention merely moved an economy further away from this state.

Rothbard believed that as a monopoly provider, any good or service provided by the government could, by definition, be more efficiently provided by the private sector. Somewhat shielded from market forces, government agents were relatively free to pursue ulterior motives at inefficient levels. In the private sector, however, competition and market forces would eliminate such inefficiencies. By questioning the legitimacy of the concept of 'government' Rothbard argued that individuals and private enterprises are capable of efficiently allocating resources, not government. Furthermore, Rothbard believed taxation to be tantamount to invoking compulsory theft onto a nation; simply an abuse of monopoly power which was used to pay for (and hence encourage) the funding of inefficient public services.

Rothbard was hugely critical of state corporatism, or 'lobbying'. As he saw it, this was quite simply corruption, with much of Rothbard's work highlighting the fundamental problems involved when corporations are able to influence public policy to favour their own personal corporate interests.

"IT'S TRUE: GREED HAS HAD A VERY BAD PRESS. I FRANKLY DON'T SEE ANYTHING WRONG WITH GREED. I THINK THAT THE PEOPLE WHO ARE ALWAYS ATTACKING GREED WOULD BE MORE CONSISTENT WITH THEIR POSITION IF THEY REFUSED THEIR NEXT SALARY INCREASE."

ROTHBARD FROM ECONOMIC CONTROVERSIES

"A ROBBER WHO JUSTIFIED HIS THEFT BY SAYING THAT HE REALLY HELPED HIS VICTIMS BY HIS SPENDING GIVING A BOOST TO RETAIL TRADE, WOULD FIND FEW CONVERTS. BUT WHEN THIS THEORY IS CLOTHED IN KEYNESIAN EQUATIONS AND IMPRESSIVE REFERENCES TO THE 'MULTIPLIER EFFECT', IT UNFORTUNATELY CARRIES MORE CONVICTION."

ROTHBARD ON TAXATION FROM ANATOMY OF THE STATE

40 EUGENE FAMA

B.1939

Is the stock market all about luck? Can anyone *really* claim to 'beat the market'? Or rather, do stock prices follow a 'random walk'?

In the 1960s, American economist Eugene Fama released a theory that was to be so influential, albeit controversial, that it has dominated many perceptions of the financial markets ever since. It is, Fama argued, impossible to consistently achieve returns in excess of market returns, in light of publicly available information.

So how does it work? Well, through his 'Efficient Market Hypothesis' (EMH), Fama proposed that three types of market efficiency exist; weak, semi-strong and strong.

In 'weakly' efficient markets, Fama proposed that asset prices already reflect all historic publicly available information (achieved from historical trends) and thus in this form they are impossible to profit from. In Fama's 'semi-strong' form, all *publicly available* information is reflected in asset prices, and thus only insider trading (i.e. trading on *private* information) is profitable. Lastly, Fama's 'strong form' emphasizes that *all* information (both private and publicly available) is reflected in asset prices, that is, insider trading doesn't even work in strong form.

With a considerable amount of evidence in favour of Fama's EMH, it came to dominate both investor and regulator attitudes for the latter half of the 20th century, with the belief in the efficiency of the market generating a relatively 'laissez-faire' financial regulatory environment. Every business school student has studied the EMH, and every financial trader has an opinion on it.

More recently, however, the credibility of the EMH has come into question, with many citing stock market bubbles and the various stock market crashes and corporate scandals as evidence for the inefficiency of markets. Numerous financial Economists have sought to disprove the EMH by referring to factors of behavioural finance that have an otherwise illogical basis in market information, but have a statistically significant, testable effect. Such examples include overconfidence, over-optimism, herding and loss aversion.

"AN INVESTOR DOESN'T HAVE A PRAYER OF PICKING A MANAGER THAT CAN DELIVER TRUE ALPHA."

EUGENE FAMA FROM FORBES

"I DON'T BELIEVE ANYONE WANTS TO HEAR WHAT I HAVE TO SAY."

FAMA IN AN INTERVIEW WITH THE NEW YORK TIMES IN 2013

41 MILTON FRIEDMAN

1912–2006

Should we legalize marijuana? Decriminalize prostitution? Milton Friedman thought so.

Born in Brooklyn in 1912 to immigrant Jewish parents, Nobel Laureate Milton Friedman was the 20th century's leading and most renowned advocate of free markets. With an unfaltering passion for economic rights and freedom, throughout his life Friedman played pivotal roles in the economic policies of Richard Nixon, Ronald Reagan and Margaret Thatcher, with the intellectual substance of his work diffusing throughout both the Federal Reserve and the Bank of England for many years.

Friedman advocated strongly for the concept of the 'free market'; opposing the contemporary Keynesian-influenced government policies and resuscitating public belief in monetary policy standing as the key determinant in achieving economic stability.

In essence, Friedman's ideas stemmed from the belief in the existence of a close and stable relationship between the money supply and price inflation, principally that monetary deflation should be employed to combat price inflation, and conversely that monetary inflation should be employed to combat price deflation. Regarding the latter, Friedman famously said that this could be achieved by simply dropping money out of a helicopter.

In his career Friedman played the role of economist, policy entrepreneur and advocate of the free-market. *The Economist* described him as "the most influential economist of the second half of the 20th century... possibly of all of it."

Friedman's papers were thought to be so powerful that they were banned in most communist countries at the time.

> "INFLATION IS ALWAYS AND EVERYWHERE A MONETARY PHENOMENON"
>
> *MILTON FRIEDMAN FROM COUNTER-REVOLUTION IN MONETARY THEORY*

Inspiring a wave of young economists from his base at The University of Chicago (including 'The Chicago Boys'), Friedman's magnum opus, *Capitalism and Freedom*, argues in favour of freely floating exchange rates and fervently outlines the case against both military conscription (seeing it as preventing young men from shaping their lives as they chose) and the welfare state (alternatively proposing a negative income tax). Should doctors be licensed? Friedman didn't think so – he warned that awarding doctors licenses decreases competition and merely encourages a monopoly of the medical industry.

FRIEDMAN WAS AN IMPORTANT MEMBER OF THE TEAM DURING WORLD WAR 2 THAT DEVELOPED A NEW PROXIMITY FUSE FOR ANTI-AIRCRAFT PROJECTILES, WHICH PREVENTED SHELLS FROM EXPLODING UNLESS THEY WERE NEAR THE OBJECT THEY ARE MEANT TO DESTROY.

"THERE IS NOT A SINGLE PERSON IN THE WORLD WHO COULD MAKE A PENCIL. REMARKABLE STATEMENT? NOT AT ALL! THE WOOD FROM WHICH IT IS MADE, FOR ALL I KNOW, COMES FROM A TREE THAT WAS CUT DOWN IN THE STATE OF WASHINGTON. TO CUT DOWN THAT TREE, IT TOOK A SAW. TO MAKE THE SAW, IT TOOK STEEL. TO MAKE STEEL IT TOOK IRON ORE. THIS BLACK CENTRE? WE CALL IT LEAD BUT ITS REALLY GRAPHITE, COMPRESSED GRAPHITE. I'M NOT SURE WHERE IT COMES FROM, BUT I THINK IT COMES FROM SOME MINES IN SOUTH AMERICA. THIS RED TOP UP HERE? IT'S RUBBER, PROBABLY FROM MALAYA, WHERE THE RUBBER TREE ISN'T EVEN NATIVE... THIS BRASS FERRULE? I HAVEN'T THE SLIGHTEST IDEA WHERE IT CAME FROM! OR THE YELLOW PAINT... OR THE GLUE THAT HOLDS IT TOGETHER.

LITERALLY THOUSANDS OF DIFFERENT PEOPLE COOPERATED TO MAKE THIS PENCIL. PEOPLE WHO DON'T SPEAK THE SAME LANGUAGE, WHO PRACTISE DIFFERENT RELIGIONS, WHO MIGHT HATE EACH OTHER IF THEY MET!...BUT WHAT BROUGHT THEM TOGETHER AND INDUCED THEM TO COOPERATE TO MAKE THIS PENCIL?... IT WAS THE MAGIC OF THE PRICE SYSTEM; THE IMPERSONAL OPERATION OF PRICES THAT BROUGHT THEM TOGETHER AND GOT THEM TO COOPERATE, TO MAKE THIS PENCIL, SO YOU COULD HAVE IT FOR A TRIFLING SUM.

THAT IS WHY THE OPERATION OF THE FREE MARKET IS SO ESSENTIAL. NOT ONLY TO PROMOTE PRODUCTIVE EFFICIENCY, BUT EVEN MORE TO FOSTER HARMONY AND PEACE AMONG THE PEOPLE OF THE WORLD."

FRIEDMAN FROM FREE TO CHOOSE

42 HARRY MARKOWITZ

B.1927

Throughout history, many have spent time attempting to develop methods and strategies that come close to 'the perfect investment'. But none has been as popular as the Nobel Prize winning economist Harry Markowitz's 1952 publication of the Modern Portfolio Theory (MPT).

Developed during his PhD at the University of Chicago, the MPT studies the effects of asset risk, return, correlation and diversification on probable investment portfolio returns, concepts which were essential to the development of the Capital Asset Pricing Model.

UPON RECEIVING HIS PHD FROM THE UNIVERSITY OF CHICAGO, THE IDEA OF THE MPT WAS SO NOVEL THAT MILTON FRIEDMAN ARGUED THAT HIS CONTRIBUTION WAS NOT EVEN ECONOMICS.

The MPT states that when making investment decisions, an understanding of 'risk' and 'return' is simply not enough. By investing in more than one stock an investor is able to enjoy the benefits of 'diversification', most importantly a reduction on the riskiness of the portfolio. Essentially, MPT applies mathematical formulations to quantify the benefits of diversification to ultimately allow the investor to manage and price risk accordingly.

Interestingly, Markowitz chose to refer to it as 'Portfolio Theory', firm in the belief that there was nothing 'modern' about it.

Nonetheless Markowitz's groundbreaking work changed the way that people invested and today, every investment manager worldwide has an understanding of his studies.

A 'MARKOWITZ EFFICIENT PORTFOLIO' IS ONE WHERE NO ADDED DIVERSIFICATION CAN LOWER THE PORTFOLIO'S RISK FOR A GIVEN RETURN EXPECTATION (ALTERNATELY, NO ADDITIONAL EXPECTED RETURN CAN BE GAINED WITHOUT INCREASING THE RISK OF THE PORTFOLIO).

"TO REDUCE RISK IT IS NECESSARY TO AVOID A PORTFOLIO WHOSE
SECURITIES ARE ALL HIGHLY CORRELATED WITH EACH OTHER. ONE
HUNDRED SECURITIES WHOSE RETURNS RISE AND FALL IN NEAR
UNISON AFFORD LITTLE PROTECTION THAN THE UNCERTAIN RETURN OF
A SINGLE SECURITY."

MARKOWITZ FROM PORTFOLIO SELECTION

43 MUHAMMAD YUNUS

B. 1940

How much money do you need to start a business?

The Nobel Peace Prize winning Bangladeshi economist Muhammad Yunus is widely credited as the creator of modern 'microcredit'. In essence, microcredit represents the provision of small (often tiny) loans to those in poverty in order to stimulate entrepreneurship.

The origins of microcredit (and more broadly microfinance) stem back to 1974, when Professor Yunus led a field trip of Chittagong University students to a local rural village. During the trip they met a local craftswoman, who had no bank account and had only a shared hut as her home. Clearly unable to get a loan from a traditional bank, they learnt that in order to buy the raw bamboo shoots she needed to craft into each piece of furniture, she had to borrow the equivalent of 15p from local lenders. On this, she paid an interest rate of approximately 10% per week, leaving her with a mere 1p profit margin. Had she been able to borrow larger amounts at more advantageous rates, she could elevate herself above her subsistence level and create a more sustainable business model.

Firm in the belief that poor households should have permanent access to not only credit, but also to savings, insurance and fund transfers, in 1983 Professor Yunus founded the Grameen Bank (taken from the term for 'rural' in Bengali), calling it the 'Bank for the Poor'.

Believing that even tiny amounts of money can generate the 'spark' required to foster enterprise and incentivize the poor to pull themselves out of poverty, Professor Yunus' findings have generated a groundswell of support, both within the finance community and beyond.

NATURALLY, BORROWERS OF MICROCREDIT ARE THOSE LACKING THE COLLATERAL, EMPLOYMENT RECORD AND SOUND CREDIT HISTORY REQUIRED TO GAIN ACCESS TO THE MORE TRADITIONAL ASPECTS OF CREDIT...

...BUT WHY THEN DOES YUNUS' BANK HAVE A RECOVERY RATE OF OVER **97%**; HIGHER THAN ANY OTHER BANKING SYSTEM IN THE WORLD?

44 NICK LEESON

B.1967

"I'm sorry" read the scribbled note on the Singaporean trading desk on 23rd February 1994. The author was recognizable.

Arrested whilst on the run at Frankfurt airport a week later, Nick Leeson proceeded to recount what was to become the biggest financial fraud of the 20th century.

Born the son of a plasterer in Watford (London), Leeson rose to become the Chief Trader in Singapore of the United Kingdom's oldest investment bank, Barings.

By the early 1990s, Leeson had become Barings' star trader; by 1993 he was responsible for 10% of the bank's profits.

A momentous lack of management judgement allowed Leeson to simultaneously act as both Chief Trader whilst also settling his own trades. As Chief Trader, from 1992 Leeson began to make unauthorized speculative trades on the Nikkei 225, initially making large profits, but soon generating large losses. To cover these losses, Leeson started using the error account 88888.

By the end of 1992, account 88888's losses totalled £2 million, but by December 1994 this had risen to over £200 million. Increasingly desperate, Leeson took a position betting that the Nikkei index would not drop below 19,000 points, a seemingly reasonable position at the time.

However on 17th January 1995, a large earthquake hit Kobe in Japan, sending the Nikkei, and Leeson's position, into a nose-dive. Requesting extra funds to continue trading, Leeson took a series of risky long, un-hedged positions; this time betting that the Nikkei would stabilize at 19,000 points. It didn't. Out of desperation, over the next three months Leeson bought over 20,000 futures contracts (worth about £180,000 each) in an attempt to move the market. It still didn't.

The US$1.3 billion of liabilities that Leeson accumulated exceeded the total capital and reserves of the bank, and the United Kingdom's oldest investment bank was declared insolvent on 26th February 1995.

BARINGS BANK WAS EVENTUALLY BOUGHT IN 1995 FOR £1 BY THE DUTCH BANK ING.

"I'M SORRY."

THE NOTE LEFT BY LEESON ON HIS DESK
SHORTLY BEFORE HE FLED SINGAPORE,
FEBRUARY 1994

45 KEN LAY

1942–2006

At 3:11am on 5th July 2006, a 64 year old man was pronounced dead at Aspen Valley Hospital. The cause of death was a heart attack and the man was Kenneth Lay, who at the time was awaiting sentencing for one of history's largest ever cases of corporate corruption and accounting fraud.

Born into a working class Baptist family, Lay rose to become one of America's highest paid CEOs, earning over $40 million in 1999 alone. During Lay's tenure, Enron transformed itself from a modest natural gas company in Omaha, into the world's leading energy corporation. Lay was a personal friend and corporate donor to George W. Bush, and was tipped as a possible contender for President Bush's Treasury secretary.

Enron was a pioneer in the energy sector. In December 2000 Senator Phil Gramm passed through legislation deregulating California's energy commodity trading. As a result, wholesale revenues quadrupled from $12 billion per quarter to approximately $50 billion.

WITH REPORTED YEARLY REVENUES OF OVER $100 BILLION IN 2000, IN 2001 ENRON WAS VOTED 'AMERICA'S MOST INNOVATIVE COMPANY' FOR THE SIXTH CONSECUTIVE YEAR. 'INNOVATIVE'? YOU BET.

Since 1993, Enron had been using a series of 'limited liability special purpose entities', within which taxes could be avoided and liabilities could be parked to make Enron appear more profitable than it actually was; thus maintaining its 'investment grade' credit status. Asset inflation was widespread, creating a vicious cycle whereby increasingly inventive and creative accounting treatments had to be employed each quarter to maintain the inflated stock price and the illusion of billions of profits that it had created for itself.

Little by little, financial analysts began to decipher Enron's lack of transparency and off-balance sheet network. As the firm began to unravel, Lay and other Enron executives defiantly urged employees to buy stock, even as they, acting on inside information, were secretly unloading their stocks and stock options. Between 1998 and 2001, Lay unloaded over $300 million of his personal shares. On 2nd December 2001, with debts of over $23 billion, Enron filed for Chapter 11 bankruptcy; the largest in US history at the time.

THE SCANDAL CAUSED THE DISSOLUTION OF ARTHUR ANDERSEN, ONE OF THE WORLD'S TOP ACCOUNTING FIRMS EMPLOYING OVER 110,000 PEOPLE WORLDWIDE.

"I TAKE FULL RESPONSIBILITY FOR WHAT HAPPENED AT ENRON ...

... BUT SAYING THAT, I KNOW IN MY MIND THAT I DID NOTHING CRIMINAL."

KEN LAY, THE NEW YORK TIMES

46 BERNARD MADOFF

B.1938

On the eve of 10th December 2008, in a palatial Upper East Side penthouse apartment, Bernard Madoff sat down with his wife and two sons and confessed to what would become known as the biggest financial fraud in history. He was "finished" he reportedly confessed, it was "just one big lie" and "basically, a giant Ponzi scheme". On 29th June 2009 Bernard Madoff was sentenced to 150 years in prison for defrauding investors of almost $65 billion through his operation of the largest Ponzi scheme in history.

Bernard L. Madoff Investment Securities LLC was founded in 1960, using an initial start-up capital of $5,000 which Madoff had earned from working primarily as a lifeguard and sprinkler installer.

Initially a market making 'penny stock' trader, Madoff dealt 'over-the-counter' with retail clients and functioned as a third market provider; bypassing exchange specialist firms. In order to compete with rivals who were members of the NYSE's floor, the firm was an early pioneer of employing computer technology to disseminate quotes, which later helped to develop the NASDAQ. Madoff is generally believed to be the first well-known practitioner of 'payment order flow', where a dealer pays a broker to influence how the broker routes client orders.

Madoff's fund offered steady but consistent returns to a largely exclusive clientele; with consistent returns around 10% per annum he found fund raising relatively easy in the golf and country clubs of Long Island and Palm Beach where his status was considered legendary. The firm grew to become the largest market maker at the NASDAQ and the sixth largest market maker on Wall Street.

However, Madoff wasn't the 'superstar' fund manager he claimed to be, and was in fact just running a Ponzi scheme – using new investors capital to repay 'profits' for existing investors.

Suspicions about Madoff's business were raised as early as 1999, focusing upon the consistently high returns that were provided by his mysterious 'wealth management' division. Tellingly perhaps, very few of the major derivatives firms traded with Madoff, in addition to several high-profile Wall Street executives not engaging with him on a professional level (despite being socially friendly with Madoff). Madoff's choice of auditors further augmented concerns; a multi-billion dollar business choosing a three-person accountancy firm.

Throughout his trial, Madoff insisted that he was solely responsible for the fraud, choosing not to cooperate with the authorities and naming no co-conspirators.

"IT'S A PROPRIETARY STRATEGY. I CAN'T GO INTO IT IN GREAT DETAIL."

MADOFF'S RESPONSE IN 2001 WHEN QUIZZED BY A JOURNALIST OVER HIS CONSISTENTLY IMPRESSIVE RETURNS FROM BARRONS

MADOFF IS CURRENTLY DUE TO BE RELEASED FROM PRISON ON 14TH NOVEMBER 2139.

47 WARREN BUFFETT

B.1930

An ambitious 14 year old boy growing up in Omaha, Nebraska declared that "if he didn't become a millionaire, he would jump off the tallest building in Omaha".

Becoming a millionaire aged 32, Warren Buffett, the 'Oracle of Omaha', stands as one of, if not *the,* greatest investors of all time. The legendary investor received his MS in Economics from Columbia Business School in 1951, studying under the guidance of the famous 'value investing' securities analyst

BUFFETT WAS REJECTED FROM HARVARD BUSINESS SCHOOL

Benjamin Graham. Buffett received the only ever A+ awarded by Graham in his securities analysis classes.

Officially beginning his career aged 21, Buffett had been making money for as long as anyone can remember. Aged six, Buffett used to buy six-packs of Coca-Cola, splitting them up to sell individually, and pocketing a small profit in the process. Aged 11, Buffett bought his first shares; six shares of Cities Service preferred. Buffett filed his first tax return at age 14, taking a $35 deduction for the use of his bicycle and watch on his paper round.

In 1956, 'Buffett Associates Ltd' was set up; a partnership created from capital of $105,000 from family and friends, and only $100 from Buffett himself. From here, Buffett went on to create one of the greatest fortunes ever amassed by an individual. Throughout his career, Buffett's most famous investments include Coca-Cola, GEICO Insurance, General Re, Goldman Sachs, *The Washington Post* and Bank of America. Now (at the time of writing) operating through Berkshire Hathaway, Buffett enjoys one of the finest reputations on Wall Street. **A critic of short-term trading, when asked of Berkshire Hathaway's optimum investing period, Buffett famously replied "our favorite holding period is forever".**

In 2008, having amassed a $73 billion fortune, *Forbes* reported Buffett to be the wealthiest man in the world. Yet Buffett still lives in the same house that he bought in 1957, drives a Cadillac DTS, and refuses to carry a mobile phone. Perhaps the greatest philanthropist of the 20th century, Buffett has pledged to give away 99% of his fortune to philanthropic causes.

"I ALWAYS KNEW I WAS GOING TO BE RICH. I DON'T THINK I EVER DOUBTED IT FOR A MINUTE."

WARREN BUFFETT FROM INSIDE THE INVESTOR'S BRAIN

"BEWARE OF GEEKS BEARING FORMULAS."

WARREN BUFFETT FROM A SHAREHOLDERS LETTER, 2008

"DERIVATIVES ARE FINANCIAL WEAPONS OF MASS DESTRUCTION."

WARREN BUFFETT FROM A SHAREHOLDERS LETTER, 2002

48 GEORGE SOROS

B.1930

"The man who broke the Bank of England" read the headlines in London in late September 1992. The man, of course, was billionaire hedge fund manager George Soros. He made over $1 billion that week (and that wasn't even his finest year).

George Soros, the Hungarian-American financier, provides one of the most moving success stories in modern finance. Soros' father was taken prisoner during World War 1, eventually fleeing captivity in Russia to be reunited with his family in Budapest. Soros was 13 years old when the Nazi's invaded Hungary and began deporting Hungarian Jews to concentration camps. Surviving the Battle of Budapest, Soros travelled to London, where he studied at the London School of Economics, funding himself by working as a railway porter and a waiter.

In 1952 Soros gained a graduate position at Singer & Friedlanders investment bank in London, and in 1956 he moved to New York to become an arbitrage trader. It was during this time that he developed his theory of 'reflexivity'. Foreseeing the opportunities that the undeveloped hedge fund industry offered, in 1973 Soros founded one of the earliest hedge funds, the 'Soros fund', with $12 million start up capital.

Later renamed the 'Quantum fund', Soros' defining moment occurred in 1992, when his fund short-sold over $10 billion worth of sterling in the belief that the UK government would withdraw from the Exchange Rate Mechanism (ERM). On the 16th September Soros' predictions proved correct, personally netting Soros over $1 billion within a week.

> "MARKETS ARE CONSTANTLY IN A STATE OF UNCERTAINTY AND FLUX AND MONEY IS MADE BY DISCOUNTING THE OBVIOUS AND BETTING ON THE UNEXPECTED."
>
> GEORGE SOROS FROM THE ERA OF UNCERTAINTY

Soros' speculation has not always been well received, however, least of all in Malaysia, where in 1997 the Malaysian Prime Minister publicly accused Soros of orchestrating the Asian financial crash (an accusation that Soros ardently denies).

Throughout his career, Soros has been an active philanthropist. No one can deny that Soros hasn't used his wealth to help others; his charitable donations to date are estimated at over $7 billion.

"WELL, YOU KNOW, I WAS A HUMAN BEING BEFORE I BECAME A BUSINESSMAN!"

GEORGE SOROS IN AN INTERVIEW WITH MARK SCHAPIRO

"OUR TOTAL POSITION BY BLACK WEDNESDAY HAD TO BE WORTH ALMOST £10 BILLION. WE PLANNED TO SELL MORE THAN THAT. IN FACT, WHEN NORMAN LAMONT SAID JUST BEFORE THE DEVALUATION THAT HE WOULD BORROW NEARLY £15 BILLION TO DEFEND STERLING, WE WERE AMUSED BECAUSE THAT WAS ABOUT HOW MUCH WE WANTED TO SELL."

SOROS, THE TIMES

49 NASSIM NICHOLAS TALEB

B.1960

Do we understand the world as well as we think we do? Do we often overestimate knowledge about rare events? Can we be fooled by false patterns?

These are the questions posed by Nassim Nicholas Taleb, perhaps the greatest ever commentator on risk in modern finance. His books on randomness, rare events and risk have become the reading list for financial market traders globally.

Taleb believes that we need to learn how to live and act in a world that we do not understand, and that our world is populated with 'black swan' events that we are unable to model or predict.

Naming it a 'black swan robust' society, Taleb advocates that we need to create a society in which we are able to withstand difficult to predict events.

Born in Lebanon, Taleb received his PhD from the University of Paris before entering the world of trading. Throughout his career Taleb has held trading positions at UBS, BNP Paribas, Bankers Trust and CS First Boston, in addition to founding the hedge fund Empirica Capital LLC and holding numerous high-profile advisory positions.

Taleb applies his beliefs to his trading strategy, pioneering 'tail risk hedging' (whereby investors are insured against severe market moves). Taleb's overriding strategy of recognizing large gains from rare events meant he would go through prolonged 'dry spells', interrupted by jackpot periods.

"UNLIKE A WELL-DEFINED, PRECISE GAME LIKE RUSSIAN ROULETTE, WHERE THE RISKS ARE VISIBLE TO ANYONE CAPABLE OF MULTIPLYING AND DIVIDING BY SIX, ONE DOES NOT OBSERVE THE BARREL OF REALITY."

TALEB FROM FOOLED BY RANDOMNESS

"A CEO'S INCENTIVE IS NOT TO LEARN, BECAUSE HE'S NOT PAID ON REAL VALUE. HE'S PAID ON COSMETIC VALUE. SO HE'S PAID TO BE NICE TO THE MERRILL LYNCH ANALYSTS OR THE WALL STREET ANALYSTS. SO THIS IS WHERE THE PROBLEM STARTS."

TALEB FROM FOOLED BY RANDOMNESS

"YOU HAVE FAMILY-OWNED BUSINESSES THAT HAVE BEEN AROUND FOR 500 YEARS. YOU CANNOT NAME A CORPORATION THAT SURVIVES INTACT FOR EVEN A FEW DECADES."

TALEB FROM THE GUARDIAN

"DON'T EVER CONFUSE LACK OF VOLATILITY WITH STABILITY, EVER."

TALEB FROM ZEROHEDGE.COM

"THE TRACK RECORD OF ECONOMISTS IN PREDICTING EVENTS IS MONSTROUSLY BAD. IT IS BEYOND SIMPLIFICATION; IT IS LIKE MEDIEVAL MEDICINE."

TALEB FROM FORBES

50 DICK FULD

B.1946

When a young, angry US air force pilot got into a brawl with his commanding officer, it was time for him to find another career. His plan B? Investment banking.

Richard 'Dick' Fuld Jnr's 39 year investment banking career began and finished at US investment banking giant Lehman Brothers.

Initially starting as a commercial paper trader, the 'gorilla of Wall Street' rapidly rose through the ranks. As a talented trader with a notorious temper, Fuld tough-talked his way to the top; eventually becoming the longest-serving CEO on Wall Street.

Under Fuld's tenure as CEO from 1994 through to the firm's collapse in 2008, Lehmans became increasingly successful; turning a $102 million loss (in 1993 – the year before he became CEO) into a $4.2 billion profit in 2007. Although reportedly feared by almost everyone who worked for him, during his time at Lehman brothers Fuld went further than any other financial boss to spread the wealth created by the business amongst his staff.

So how did it all go wrong? It's hard to say for certain, although Fuld certainly underestimated the effect that the downturn in the US housing market would have on the firm's mortgage bond underwriting business. Even in the bank's dying months, Fuld's notorious ego refused to acknowledge that they were in trouble; "as long as I am alive this firm will never be sold!" reported *The Wall Street Journal*. By the time Fuld acknowledged the banks imminent demise, Lehmans was finished.

At 1am on 15th September 2008, Lehman Brothers Holdings announced it would be filing for the largest bankruptcy in history, citing bank debts of $613 billion.

BETWEEN 1993 AND 2007 FULD RECEIVED ALMOST $500 MILLION IN TOTAL COMPENSATION.

IN 2006 *INSTITUTIONAL INVESTOR* NAMED FULD AMERICA'S TOP CEO.

DURING AN INTERNAL LEHMAN BROTHERS CONFERENCE IN 2007, WHEN ASKED OF HIS STRATEGY REGARDING THE SHORT-SELLING OF LEHMAN STOCK, FULD PROUDLY ANNOUNCED:

"... WHAT I REALLY WANT TO DO, IS I WANT TO REACH IN, RIP OUT THEIR HEART, AND EAT IT BEFORE THEY DIE!"

GLOSSARY

ACCOUNTING The Medici Family, Ken Lay, Bernard Madoff, Michael Milken.

AMERICA Amadeo P. Giannini, Charles Ponzi, J.P. Morgan, Franklin D. Roosevelt, Waddill Catchings, Hetty Green, John von Neumann, Harry Dexter White, Sidney Weinberg, Georges Doriot, Benjamin Graham, Alfred Winslow Jones, Peter Drucker, Ronald Reagan, Bernard Cornfeld, Robert Vesco, Hyman Minsky, Michael Milken, Murray Rothbard, Eugene Fama, Milton Friedman, Ken Lay, Bernard Madoff, Warren Buffett, Dick Fuld.

ARBITRAGE Charles Ponzi, George Soros, The Rothschild Family.

AUSTRIAN SCHOOL OF ECONOMICS F.A. Hayek, Ludwig von Mises, Murray Rothbard.

AUTOCRACY Chanakya.

BANKING Amadeo P. Giannini, The Medici Family, The Knights Templar, Muhammad Yunus.

BANKING DYNASTY The Medici Family, The Rothschild Family, J.P. Morgan.

BRITAIN John Law, Sir John Blunt, John Maynard Keynes, Charles Hall, Nick Leeson, The Knights Templar, Adam Smith, David Ricardo, Benjamin Graham.

CENTRAL BANKING Alves dos Reis, Milton Friedman, Franklin D. Roosevelt, Ronald Reagan, John Maynard Keynes, Harry Dexter White.

CHEQUES The Knights Templar.

CHINA Deng Xiaoping.

COMMUNISM Karl Marx, Deng Xiaoping.

CREATIVE DESTRUCTION Joseph Schumpeter.

CREDIT The Knights Templar, Michael Milken, Amadeo P. Giannini.

ECONOMICS Adam Smith, David Ricardo, Vilfredo Pareto, F.A. Hayek, John von Neumann, Joseph Schumpeter, Hyman Minsky, Chanakya, John Maynard Keynes, Harry Dexter White, Murray Rothbard, Eugene Fama, Ludwig von Mises, Milton Friedman, Ken Lay.

ENTREPRENEUR Joseph Schumpeter, Warren Buffett, Georges Doriot, Bernard Cornfeld, Robert Vesco, Muhammad Yunus, John Law, Sir John Blunt, Amadeo P. Giannini, J.P. Morgan.

ESPIONAGE Harry Dexter White.

FINANCIAL INNOVATION The Rothschild Family, Bernard Cornfeld, Ken Lay, Waddill Catchings, Henry Kravis, Michael Milken, Muhammad Yunus.

FRANCE Nicole Oresme, The Medici Family, John Law, Bernard Cornfeld.

FREE MARKET Adam Smith, Milton Friedman, Ronald Reagan, F.A. Hayek, Joseph Schumpeter, Ludwig von Mises, Murray Rothbard.

FORGERY Charles Ponzi, Alves dos Reis, Robert Vesco, Ken Lay, Hetty Green.

HARVARD Harry Dexter White, Georges Doriot, Hyman Minsky, Joseph Schumpeter, Franklin D. Roosevelt, Waddill Catchings.

HEDGE FUNDS Alfred Winslow Jones, George Soros, Warren Buffett.

INDIA Chanakya, Muhammad Yunus.

INVESTMENT Hetty Green, Warren Buffett, George Soros, Robert Vesco, The Rothschild Family, Georges Doriot, Harry Markowitz.

INVESTMENT BANKING J.P. Morgan, Sidney Weinberg, George Soros, Henry Kravis, Michael Milken, Dick Fuld, Nick Leeson.

INNOVATION Joseph Schumpeter, Georges Doriot, Henry Kravis, Michael Milken.

JEWISH The Rothschild Family, Bernard Madoff, Milton Friedman, Murray Rothbard, Bernard Cornfeld, David Ricardo, Karl Marx, Ludwig von Mises, Sidney Weinberg, Bernard Cornfeld, George Soros, Benjamin Graham, Dick Fuld, Harry Dexter White, Hyman Minsky, Michael Milken, Harry Markowitz.

JOURNALISM Alfred Winslow Jones.

LEVERAGE Alfred Winslow Jones, Waddill Catchings, Henry Kravis, Nick Leeson, Hyman Minsky, Michael Milken, Robert Vesco, George Soros.

MANAGEMENT CONSULTING Peter Drucker.

MUTUAL FUNDS Bernard Cornfeld, Robert Vesco, Harry Markowitz.

OPTIONS Thales of Miletus, Nick Leeson.

PHILANTHROPY Henry Kravis, Warren Buffett, Amadeo P. Giannini, The Rothschild Family, The Medici Family, Charles Hall, Michael Milken, George Soros, J.P. Morgan.

PONZI SCHEME John Law, Bernard Madoff, Charles Ponzi, Hyman Minsky.

PRIVATE EQUITY Georges Doriot, Henry Kravis, J.P. Morgan, Michael Milken.

PRIVATIZATION Ronald Reagan, Milton Friedman, Deng Xiaoping.

QUANTITY THEORY OF MONEY Nicole Oresme, Milton Friedman, Franklin D. Roosevelt, John Maynard Keynes, F.A. Hayek.

SOCIALISM Charles Hall, Karl Marx, Deng Xiaoping.

STOCK MARKET BUBBLE John Law, Sir John Blunt, George Soros, Nassim Nicholas Taleb, Hyman Minsky, Waddill Catchings, Eugene Fama.

STOCK MARKET INVESTING The Rothschild Family, Benjamin Graham, Warren Buffett, J.P. Morgan, George Soros, Nick Leeson, Bernard Cornfeld, Michael Milken, Eugene Fama, Nassim Nicholas Taleb, Waddill Catchings, Hetty Green, Hyman Minsky, Nick Leeson, Harry Markowitz.

TRADE UNIONS Karl Marx, Ronald Reagan.

VATICAN The Medici Family.

VENTURE CAPITAL Georges Doriot.

1929 WALL STREET CRASH Franklin D. Roosevelt, Waddill Catchings, J.P. Morgan.

REFERENCES

Adams, T. (2010) Nassim Taleb: 'Big corporations will always fail', *The Guardian*, 20 June.

Ante, S.E. (2008) *Creative Capital: Georges Doriot and the Birth of Venture Capital*, Harvard Business Review Press.

Aristotle (2009) *The Politics of Aristotle: A Treatise on Government*, The Floating Press.

Arvedlund, E. (2001) Don't Ask, Don't Tell: Bernie Madoff Attracts Skeptics in 2001, *Barrons*, 7 May, http://online.barrons.com/articles/SB989019667829349012.

Baltzell, E.D. (1987) *The Protestant Establishment: Aristocracy and Caste in America,* Yale University Press.

Barge, P. (2006) *The Little Book of Big Decisions,* John Wiley & Sons.

Berkshire Hathaway (1988) Shareholders letter, http://www.berkshirehathaway.com/letters/1988.html.

Berkshire Hathaway (2002) Shareholders letter, http://www.berkshirehathaway.com/letters/2002pdf.pdf.

Berkshire Hathaway (2008) Shareholders letter, http://www.berkshirehathaway.com/letters/2008ltr.pdf.

Calder, J. (1995) Obituaries: Bernie Cornfeld, *The Independent*, 1 March, http://www.independent.co.uk/news/people/obituaries--bernie-cornfeld-1609472.html.

Craig, S., McCracken, J., Lucchetti, A. and Kelly, K. (2008) The Weekend That Wall Street Died, *The Wall Street Journal*, 29 December, http://www.wsj.com/articles/SB123051066413538349.

Darby, M. (1998) In Ponzi We Trust, *Smithsonian Magazine*, December.

Das, S. (2012) So how long can the US hold the world to ransom with the dollar?, *The Independent*, 24 October, http://www.independent.co.uk/news/business/comment/satyajit-das-so-how-long-can-the-us-hold-the-world-to-ransom-with-the-dollar-8223577.html.

Drucker, P. (1946) *Concept of the Corporation*, John Day.

Drucker, P. (1992) *Managing the Non-Profit Organization: Principles and Practices*, Collins.

Eichenwald, K. (2004) Crimes of Others Wrecked Enron, Ex-Chief Says, *The New York Times*, 27 June.

Efrati, A. Lauricella, T. and Searcey, D. (2008) Top Broker Accused of $50 Billion Fraud, *The Wall Street Journal*, 12 December, http://www.wsj.com/articles/SB122903010173099377.

Ellis, C.D. (2009) *The Partnership: The Making of Goldman Sachs*, Penguin Books.

Evans, R. (2014) How (not) to invest like Sir Isaac Newton, *The Telegraph*, 23 May, http://www.telegraph.co.uk/finance/personalfinance/investing/10848995/How-not-to-invest-like-Sir-Isaac-Newton.html.

Ferguson, N. (2012) History of Money and Banking, *Philosophy, Politics and Economics*, 2 July, http://philosophyeconomicsandpolitics.blogspot.co.uk/2012/07/ascent-of-money.html.

Fisher, D. (2012) Eugene Fama on Inflation, the Crisis, and Why You Can't Beat the Market After Fees, *Forbes*, 2 December.

Ford, C. (1905) Hetty Green: A Character Study, *National Magazine*, September.

Fortune (2004) The Man Who Changed Medicine, 29 November, http://archive.fortune.com/magazines/fortune/fortune_archive/2004/11/29/8192713/index.htm.

Friedman, M. (1962) *Capitalism and Freedom*, University of Chicago Press.

Friedman, M. (1970) *Counter-Revolution in Monetary Theory*, Institute of Economic Affairs.

Friedman, M. and Friedman, R. (1980) *Free to Choose*, TV show, http://en.wikipedia.org/wiki/Free_to_Choose.

Galbraith, J.K. (1954) *The Great Crash 1929*, Hamish Hamilton.

Gillard, M. (2008) Robert Vesco: Fugitive American financier responsible for one of the biggest frauds in history, *The Guardian*, 21 May, http://www.theguardian.com/world/2008/may/21/internationalcrime.usa.

Graham, B. (1986) *The Intelligent Investor: A Book of Practical Counsel*, 4th edition, Harpers & Row Publishers.

Gupta, U. (2004) *The First Venture Capitalist: Georges Doriot on Leadership, Capital and Business Organization*, Gondolier.

Hall, C. (1849) *The Effects of Civilization on the People in European States*, Longman.

Hayek, F.A. (1944) *The Road to Serfdom*, George Routledge & Sons.

Hayek, F.A. (1960) *The Constitution of Liberty*, Routledge.

Hayek, F.A. (1976) *The Denationalization of Money*, Institute of Economic Affairs.

Haynes, J.E., Klehr, H. and Vassiliev, A. (2009) *Spies: The Rise and Fall of the KGB in America*, Yale University Press.

Kautalya (Chanakya) (1992) *The Arthashashtra*, Penguin Books India.

Keynes, J.M. (1931) *Essays in Persuasion*, Harcourt, Brace and Company.

Keynes, J.M. (1936) *The General Theory of Employment, Interest and Money*, Palgrave.

Langreth, R. (2009) The Oracle of Doom, *Forbes*, 15 January.

Leuchtenburg, W.E. (1963) *Franklin D. Roosevelt and the New Deal, 1932–1940*, Harper & Row.

Litterick, D. (2002) The Man Who Broke the Bank of England, *The Telegraph*, 13 September, http://www.telegraph.co.uk/finance/2773265/Billionaire-who-broke-the-Bank-of-England.html.

Machiavelli, N. (2012) *The Prince*, CreateSpace Independent Publishing Platform.

Markowitz, H.M. (1971) *Portfolio Selection: Efficient Diversification of Investments*, Yale University Press.

Marx, K. (2011) *Das Kapital*, CreateSpace Independent Publishing Platform.

Marx, K. and Engels, F. (1848) *The Communist Manifesto* (originally titled *Manifesto of the Communist Party*), Workers' Educational Association.

Miles, R.P. (2004) *Warren Buffett Wealth: Principles and Practical Methods Used by the World's Greatest Investor*, John Wiley & Sons, Inc.

Mustapha, A. (1998) *Lessons From Expert Traders: The tactics, behaviour and mindset that can be learned from the world's most successful financial traders*, Harriman House Limited.

O'Neill, J. (2003) *The Market: Ethics, Knowledge and Politics*, Routledge.

Oppenheimer, F. (1941) Charles Hall: An Early Land Reformer, *The Freeman*, October.

Peterson, R.L. (2007) *Inside the Investor's Brain: The Power of Mind over Money*, John Wiley & Sons, Inc.

Povaly, S. (2010) *Private Equity Exits: Divestment Process Management for Leveraged Buyouts*, Springer.

Raw, C., Page, B. and Hodgson, G. (1971) *Do You Sincerely Want to be Rich?: The Full Story of Bernard Cornfeld and I.O.S.*, Viking Press, Inc.

Ricardo, D. (1817) *On the Principles of Political Economy and Taxation*, John Murray.

Rothbard, M. (2011) *Economic Controversies*, Ludwig von Mises Institute.

Rothbard, M. (2013) *Anatomy of the State*, lulu.com.

Russell, B. (1945) *The History of Western Philosophy*, Simon & Schuster.

Schapiro, M. (2000) Interview with George Soros, Chairman, Soros Fund Management, 5 September, http://www.simulconference.com/clients/sowf/interviews/interview3.html.

Schumpeter, J. (1942) *Capitalism, Socialism and Democracy*, Harper & Brothers.

Shaxson, N. (2012) *Treasure Islands: Tax Havens and the Men who Stole the World*, Vintage.

Shilling, A.G. (1993) Scoreboard, *Forbes*, 151(4), 15 February.

Smith, A. (1776) *The Wealth of Nations*, W. Strahan and T. Cadell.

Sommer, J. (2013) Eugene Fama, King of Predictable Markets, *The New York Times*, 26 October, http://www.nytimes.com/2013/10/27/business/eugene-fama-king-of-predictable-markets.html?_r=0.

Stein, G. (2010) Managing People and Organizations: Peter Drucker's Legacy, Emerald Group Publishing.

Taleb, N.N. (2007) *Fooled by Randomness: The Hidden Role of Chance in Life and the Markets*, Penguin.

The Economist (2006) A heavyweight champ, at five foot two: The legacy of Milton Friedman, a giant among economists, 23 November, http://www.economist.com/node/8313925.

The Times (1992) George Soros 26 October.

Trahan, F. and Krantz, K. (2011) The Era of Uncertainty: Global Investment Strategies for Inflation, Deflation and the Middle Ground, John Wiley & Sons, Inc.

Von Mises, L. (1922) *Socialism: An Economic and Sociological Analysis*, Gustav Fischer Verlag.

Von Mises, L. (1949) *Human Action: A Treatise on Economics*, Yale University Press.

Von Mises, L. (1998) *Interventionism, an Economic Analysis*, Foundation for Economic Education.

Von Neumann, J. (1958) *The Computer and the Brain*, Yale University Press.

Wall Street Journal (1926) Can You Afford a Yacht?, 14 September.

Weikal-Beauchat, W. (2013) *Courage for the Journey: Wisdom for the Broken Road*, AuthorHouse.

Wister, O. (1930) Roosevelt: The Story of a Friendship, Macmillan.

Zupan, M. (2014) All Eyes Should be on Volatility, 12 August, http://www.zerohedge.com/news/2014-08-12/all-eyes-should-be-volatility.